D0659039

Marketing Your Value

Marketing Your Value

9 Steps to Navigate Your Career

Michael Edmondson, PhD

 BUSINESS EXPERT PRESS

Marketing Your Value: 9 Steps to Navigate Your Career
Copyright © Business Expert Press, LLC, 2015.

All rights reserved. No part of this publication may be reproduced, stored in a retrieval system, or transmitted in any form or by any means—electronic, mechanical, photocopy, recording, or any other except for brief quotations, not to exceed 400 words, without the prior permission of the publisher.

First published in 2015 by   ·
Business Expert Press, LLC
222 East 46th Street, New York, NY 10017
www.businessexpertpress.com

ISBN-13: 978-1-63157-218-0 (paperback)
ISBN-13: 978-1-63157-219-7 (e-book)

Business Expert Press Human Resource Management and Organizational Behavior Collection

Collection ISSN: 1946-5637 (print)
Collection ISSN: 1946-5645 (electronic)

Cover and interior design by S4Carlisle Publishing Services Private Ltd., Chennai, India

First edition: 2015

10 9 8 7 6 5 4 3 2 1

Printed in the United States of America

Dedication

To Lori, Amanda, and Jonathan

Abstract

Marketing your value is relevant for professionals from recent college graduates to senior executives. Today's chaotic global marketplace presents new challenges with each passing day that only the most savvy of professionals will be able to navigate. Global unemployment and underemployment, the digital revolution, and technological advancements are just three of the many dynamics driving today's economy where we have to rethink how we live, work, communicate, and do just about everything else. Navigating the chaos requires a sophisticated strategy that is built upon the paradigm that professional development is directly linked to personal growth. To grow as a professional, therefore, one must increase their self-awareness, build a compelling brand, and then communicate their message in a clear and consistent fashion. *Marketing Your Value: 9 Steps to Navigate Your Career* explains how professionals can market their value to navigate their career and live a life of purpose. Divided into three sections, this publication offers you an opportunity to assess your personal and professional skills, challenges you to create a compelling personal brand, and helps you develop the communication materials necessary to navigate your career. This Assess, Brand, Communicate (ABC) approach is relevant for undergraduates, recent college graduates, graduate students, entry level professionals, experienced managers, and senior leaders across the globe. Each of the nine steps included in this publication will challenge you to think deeply to increase your self-awareness. With ubiquitous technology surrounding your eyes and ears 24/7, you have few moments of quiet to afford the time for self-reflection. Yet this is an absolute necessity if you are to successfully market your value and navigate your career.

Key word sampling

marketing, career development, employment, communication, personal development, professional development

Advanced quotes for *Marketing Your Value: 9 Steps to Navigate Your Career*

Dr. Edmondson provides graduates and professionals with a road map to bring to practice Jonathan Winters' quote, "If your ship doesn't come in, swim out to meet it." Not only does he make a compelling case for swimming to meet the ship, he also provides readers with the knowledge of how to swim, and to swim in the right direction: the "Assess, Brand, and Communicate" approach. This book is an excellent read for college students, recent graduates and mid-career professionals as they navigate their careers and prepare for the next step towards their professional goals.

Pareena Lawrence, PhD.
Provost and Dean of the College
Professor of Economics
Augustana College, Rock Island, Illinois

Michael Edmondson brings many years of advising emerging undergraduates on the challenges and practical strategies for launching and adapting a career in a rapidly-changing global economy. While giving substantial attention to self-marketing in a digital age, Edmondson's approach is founded self-evaluation--very much in the liberal-arts tradition--asking readers to assess their values and abilities in relation to opportunities and to regard the job search as a flexible, ever-changing process of self-exploration and assessment more than orientation to a fixed goal. In the tradition of *What Color is Your Parachute* and *What Should I Do With My Life?*, *Marketing Your Value: 9 Steps to Navigate Your Career* is likely to be invaluable to anyone who is entering the job market, considering a change of direction, or advising those who are.

William Pannapacker, PhD.
Professor of English
Director of the Andrew W. Mellon Foundation Scholars Program in the
Arts and Humanities,
Faculty Director of the Great Lakes Colleges Association's Digital
Liberal Arts Initiative.
Hope College

Michael asks the tough and provoking questions that many of us struggle with on a day-to-day basis, such as understanding our personal mission, unveiling our distractions, and coming to terms with the major influence we have in our career development. This book provides an opportunity for professionals from any age, background, and industry the time to understand themselves through a series of thoughtful and challenging reflections and activities. By doing this, Michael guides us back to our core to help us rediscover our values and use this knowledge as the foundation to successfully navigate a meaningful, and purposeful career.

Yalitza M. Negron, M.S. Ed.
Associate Director, Office of Academic Community Engagement
Siena College

Marketing Your Value: 9 Steps to Navigate Your Career is an outstanding read and is applicable to any working individual's life. Dr. Edmondson's writing is clear, concise, and informative; a true reflection of the hardships many professionals, both young and old, face in today's highly competitive workforce. Through its various exercises and practices, Marketing Your Value will help anyone understand the tools, habits, and behaviors that are necessary when traveling the road to success. Dr. Edmondson has played an integral role in the launch of my career and continues to provide me with valuable insight along my professional journey. His immense knowledge on the topics of marketing and branding clearly shines through in this publication.

Emily Nemeth
Admissions Manager of Ladywood High School (Livonia, MI)

"Marketing Your Value is a practical resource filled with helpful tools and interesting anecdotes for assessing, branding, and communicating one's value -- a valuable resource for anyone making a transition. I look forward to sharing it with my students."

Steve VanderVeen, PhD.
Director of the Center for Faithful Leadership at Hope College
Professor of Management.

"A practical book that illustrates how to successfully navigate career challenges in today's economy"

Sheila Curran,
President, Curran Consulting Group and author of Smart Moves for
Liberal Arts Grads: Finding a Path to Your Perfect Career

Contents

Foreword

You are holding an awesome tool in your hand. *Marketing Your Value* is an insightful book that can help you understand and market your value to the world. It may seem that the value you can bring to an employer is obvious because of a degree you hold or a college you graduated from or your past experiences. In today's marketplace, however, there is a lot of competition with millions of people who hold degrees and have valuable past experiences. What seems obvious to you is often lost in the sea of competition. This is a large problem for people in today's job market. The only way to address that challenge is for you to take intentional and targeted action to help others clearly see the value you offer to them.

My own journey provides an example. Holding a graduate degree in history I was searching for a job early in my career. Knowing that there are few jobs that actually ask for a history degree I decided to assess my skills and understand what I might have to offer an employer. That process led me to realize that I knew how to locate and compile information, identify trends, and write compelling reports to explain what it all meant. It became clear that I had should present myself as a researcher rather than limit myself as a historian.

I applied for a job at a marketing research company where it was not as obvious to them that a history student could be an effective marketing researcher in the pharmaceutical industry. It took convincing on my part to communicate the value of my research skills. This book would have certainly helped me through that process. When I was asked if I had any sales experience I pointed to several activities I was involved with that required me to persuade a group of people based on the research I had done. I described how I could analyze and synthesize information. They immediately saw that connection and I went on to have a very successful marketing research career until I decided to rebrand myself and move on to new challenges.

As you can see from my own experience, it is critical to assess your skills and experience, understand what it means and build a brand around it, and then communicate it effectively to potential employers. If you are like most people today you will have multiple jobs over your career; it will be a continuing process. This book will help you be successful in this effort but it requires work on your part.

Blueprints do not build a house, carpenters with hammers and saws do. *Marketing Your Value* is about taking action to achieve your professional goals. It can provide you with the hammers and saws but *you* need to put them to work. Using this workbook is your first step. With the increase in globalization and competition it is likely you will return to it again and again in the future.

Peter Abramo, PhD., CEcD
Director of the Center for Entrepreneurship
College of Wooster

Preface

I recently facilitated a workshop for undergraduates that the organizer entitled: "Landing Your Dream Job." The title immediately sparked several questions. What exactly is a dream job? Are college students aware of the dynamics driving today's global marketplace that can impact their dreams? Working off of the assumption that your dreams evolve over time, how can one land a dream job amidst lifelong personal growth and professional development? These questions and more raced through my mind. Despite my reservations I held the workshop and challenged students to do two things. First, they needed to make a commitment to never stop dreaming. Since one has the capacity to have more than one dream they should think about having more than one dream job. Determining your dream job at 18 or 22 is completely overwhelming. It is also unnecessary and unrealistic. I reminded students that far too many experienced professionals have stopped dreaming due to the pressures, commitments, and unforeseen circumstances of life.

The second thing I challenged the group of 100 college students to do was focus on what they wanted to do immediately after graduation. All too often students think they have the answer the question: "What do I want to do with the rest of my life?" This is absolutely the wrong question to answer. The right question to answer, or some variation of it, is "What do I want to do next?" or "What opportunities are before me and how do I take advantage of them to grow both personally and professionally?" The workshop developed into a conversation that anything in life is possible. What I told the crowd holds true for more experienced professionals. Continue to dream as you get older. Amidst the responsibilities of caring for children, parents, or other loved ones, it is important to take even the smallest of steps to translate your dream into reality. The caveat, of course, is that you must be willing to work hard at translating your dream into reality. As Jonathan Winters wrote, "If your ship doesn't come in, swim out to meet it." Doing so is a prerequisite in today's hypercompetitive and ever changing economy.

Global unemployment and underemployment trends represent significant issues to anyone who wants to launch or navigate their career. According to the International Labor Organization, "almost 202 million people were unemployed in 2013 around the world, an increase of almost 5 million compared with the year before."[1] The number of global employment opportunities is failing to keep pace with the growing labor force. One group facing a herculean challenge to navigate their career is young professionals. In the United States, almost half of the recent college graduates are underemployed.[2] While underemployment is high in the United States, in some countries unemployment for young professionals is catastrophic. For example, 75 million people aged 15 to 24 are jobless around the world, with youth unemployment in parts of the Middle East and North Africa at 25 percent, while in Spain and South Africa it is 50 percent.[3] During the last decade in China, "the wage premium paid to college graduates fell by 19 percentage points while unemployment among recent college graduates has risen to over 16 percent."[4] Such high levels of unemployment and underemployment, however, are just a few characteristics of today's global economy.

Another characteristic of today's world is the element of change. Change is happening at an unprecedented speed and on a far-reaching scale. While change has always been a part of life, "technology snuck up on us in the last 15 years and we now have screen sharing using WebEx, coordinating to-do lists using Basecamp, real-time chatting using instant message, and downloading the latest files with Dropbox."[5] Today's digital revolution presents new challenges on a daily basis that test our ability to adapt to it. As authors Alvin and Heidi Toffler noted, "with every passing semi-second, the accuracy of our knowledge about our investments, our markets, and our customers' need diminishes."[6] In short, the convergence of technological advancements and dynamics driving today's global marketplace have forever altered the way we live and work. To help professionals understand how to market their value and navigate such chaos, however, traditional career development strategies provide little support.

As a result of these and other dynamics driving today's economy, professionals across the globe have a tremendous need for a practical, step by step guide they can immediately implement so as to adapt to today's challenges. *Marketing Your Value: 9 Steps to Navigate Your Career* fills that gap. Divided into three sections, this publication will help you understand how to assess your personal and professional skills, build a compelling personal brand, and communicate your value. I developed this assess, brand, communicate (ABC) approach to navigating your career while teaching undergraduate students and conducting workshops for professionals across different industries during the last decade. Each step builds upon the previous one and guides you through a process of reflection to increase your self-awareness. Doing so is the prerequisite of marketing your value and navigating your career.

Why You Should Read This Book?

This book is for anyone interested in learning how to launch or navigate their career. Undergraduates, recent college graduates, graduate students, and young professionals will learn what questions to ask as they take the early steps of a long and prosperous career. More experienced professionals will encounter questions and exercises that will cause them to reflect where they are in life and chart the next step of their career path. The list below includes 15 of the many reasons why you should complete the exercises in this publication. You should read this book if you want to:

1. Advocate for yourself.
2. Understand how to better prepare yourself for tomorrow's challenges.
3. Recognize new opportunities both personally and professionally.
4. Increase your self-awareness so as to live a happier life.
5. Develop a better sense of purpose in your professional life.
6. Identify and capitalize on your cognitive and emotional strengths.
7. Launch your career.
8. Make a career change.
9. Discover new and valuable ways to discuss your experiences.
10. Assess your personal traits and habits.
11. Create a compelling personal brand based on your acquired skills.
12. Develop a clear, concise, and compelling message.
13. Start the process of marketing your value.
14. Think differently about possible career options.
15. Learn how to communicate your value offline and online.

It is important to remind yourself that amidst today's chaotic global marketplace, people are translating their dreams into reality. Achieving and sustaining a rewarding career path is possible as the "social media and digital revolution has sparked a new level of adaptability, flexibility, and opportunity" that individuals can embrace if they wish to adapt to the twists and turns life throws their way.[7]

How to Use This Book

This workbook contains exercises, questions, and audits. Each task is designed to help increase your self-awareness. Navigating your career requires you to develop as a professional and that, in turn, demands that you grow as a person. Developing the link between professional development and personal growth can help you achieve and sustain a successful career path in today's chaotic ocean of a global marketplace. While each chapter can be completed as a standalone topic, it is imperative that you complete all nine steps. Doing so will provide you with the strongest level of support as you navigate your career. You may want to have a notebook handy as there are numerous questions to answer, exercises to complete, and assessments to conduct.

You should be able to read this book in 2 or 3 hours. To answer the questions and complete the exercises, however, it will require additional time as you learn how to market your value and navigate your career. Some of the exercises require just a few minutes to complete while others require a more substantial investment of time. Understand that these nine steps represent a cycle that you can often revisit. Every so often challenge yourself to reexamine questions and exercises. Do your answers evolve over time? At the very least you should challenge yourself once a year to answer a few of the questions or exercises you found particularly appealing. We set aside so little time for self-reflection in today's world of ubiquitous communication, information, and technology that we often lose sight of our value, our purpose, and our career path. Make marketing your value and navigating your career a priority in your life and set aside the time you need to engage in self-reflection. I wish you well along your journey.

Acknowledgments

Many people have helped me navigate my career. First and foremost I need to thank Peter Abramo. We met in graduate school and have remained friends for over 24 years. With countless discussions between us, there has been no one outside of my family more supportive throughout my career. Peter is a man of outstanding character who has served his country as a Marine, is a father and husband to a wonderful family, and is an accomplished leader within economic development and higher education. I am honored to call him my friend.

Early on my career, I received help from Bill McMackin who awarded me a West Catholic Alumni scholarship to attend college. As a first generation student, this scholarship proved instrumental in allowing me to attend Cabrini College. My fellow West Catholic brothers and sisters still support me regardless of the distance or time between us, especially Randy Duck, Ed Hughes, John O'Connor, Larry Healey, John Waters, and Desiree McGarry Campbell. I would also like to acknowledge my professors at Cabrini College, Villanova University, and Temple University. Specifically I would like to thank Jolyon P. Girard, James Hedtke, and Lowell Gustafson. Your advice over the years has proven invaluable. Former Albion College President Donna Randall deserves special acknowledgment for nominating me into the Council of Independent College's Senior Leadership Academy, a catalyst for my career.

For the thousands of students I have had the pleasure of teaching over the years, I thank you. Special recognition needs to go to those students who are now friends: Emily Nemeth, Meghan Houston, Karen Siren Martin, Jelena Radmanovic, Elizabeth Clark, Allie Strandmark, Nicole Kay, John Clark, Lisa Pfeiffer Jones, and Carrie Solar. Conversations in and out of the classroom and over the years have enlightened me to the concerns you have expressed about navigating your own careers. Thank you for seeking my counsel and helping me understand the world from your view.

Thanks also to Rosa Aaron, Angel Rodriquez, Chris Aranosian, Tracy Brandenburg, Tom Bryant, Chris Cosentino, Sheila Curran, Jane Donohue, John and Janet LaFrance, Chris Nemeth, Gerard O' Sullivan, Vicki Baker Harris, Anita Martino, Rosina Miller, Erik Marero, Tony Noel, William Pannapacker, Laura Roselli, Neal Sobania, Karen and Bob Sauselein, Marie Walker and Michelle Williams. To maintain mental clarity and focus during the last 5 years I started practicing yoga and would like to thank my yoga teachers and friends, especially Kelly and Evan Harris and fellow yogis at Tapas Yoga Shala in Rock Island, Illinois. To the entire team at Business Expert Press, especially Stewart Mattson and Rob Zwettler, I owe my deepest gratitude in publishing this book.

To my current family at Augustana College in Rock Island, Illinois, thank you to the Board of Trustees, alumni, students, faculty, staff, and administration including President Steve Bahls and Provost Pareena Lawrence. To the entire staff of the Careers/Opportunities /Research/ Exploration (CORE) Center and especially the Career Development office, I owe my deepest appreciation for all of your work and support that you demonstrate on a daily basis. My Career Development staff work hard at helping students understand how to market their value and launch their career in today's chaotic global marketplace and it is an honor to serve as their leader. Additionally, Augustana's Associate Dean and Director of Institutional Research, Mark Salisbury deserves special recognition for his constant guidance and support.

Finally, I would like to acknowledge my family including Vicki and Pete Peterson, Michelle and Scott Edmondson. My wife Lori, children Amanda and Jonathan, and parents Lillian and Bernard provided tremendous inspiration and support along my journey. As a first generation college student I was very fortunate to have a mother and father who supported their son along an unfamiliar path. Without hesitation they were with me every step of the way and I am forever grateful for their love and support. Lori and I met as undergraduates and have been together now for close to 30 years. If there was a Nobel Prize for patience and understanding, Lori would deserve it since she is continually challenged to demonstrate new levels of both traits with me on a daily basis. Our children are the two brightest stars in the sky. Rest assured that my concern over your future, and that of your entire generation, formed the foundation upon which this book was written. My greatest hope is that you both learn to market your value and live with purpose as you navigate your career amidst the chaos. This book is dedicated to Lori, Amanda, and Jonathan, for without them my career would lack all navigation and my life would be void of all value and purpose. Thank you for your love and support.

Our deepest fear is not that we are inadequate. Our deepest fear is that we are powerful beyond measure. It is our light, not our darkness that most frightens us. Playing small does not serve the world. There is nothing enlightened about shrinking so that other people won't feel insecure around you. We are all meant to shine . . . And as we let our own light shine, we unconsciously give other people permission to do the same. As we are liberated from our own fear, our presence automatically liberates others.

Marianne Williams, *A Return to Love*[8]

Introduction:
Think Differently

During 2004 to 2014 the world witnessed the emergence of cloud computing, robotics, 4G wireless connectivity, crowdsourcing, social media, tablets, wearable technology, and Internet-enabled smartphones. In a world where three billion are connected via the Internet and seven billion people have mobile-cellular subscriptions,[9] we have gone from the "connected to hyperconnected"[10] in a very brief period of time. Perhaps nowhere is this shift from a connected to a hyperconnected global economy more profound than with the digital revolution and social media. Advancements in technology, the emergence of new social media platforms, and the subsequent adaptation by billions around the world continue have completely disrupted the way people work, interact with one another, present ideas, and share information. With approximately 40 percent of the world's population, or 2.7 billion people, using social media on a regular basis, the need to think differently on just about everything will only continue.[11] In today's digital revolution it is imperative to understand "that you are no longer the only one in control of your résumé."[12]

The growing ubiquity of social media and the emergence of new technologies and markets will continue to accelerate our need to think differently to adapt to the upcoming changes. Amidst today's ongoing disruptive developments it is important to remind ourselves that "the truth about change is that we tend to overestimate its speed while underestimating its reach."[13] To be clear, the reach of change and its impact on work has arrived in every corner of the globe. To succeed in this hyper-change environment you need to increase your self-awareness, engage in experiences that create a sense of disequilibrium, pursue unfamiliar horizons, and challenge yourself to think differently on just about everything.[14] But thinking differently, and moving away from the usual approach to life and work is a formidable challenge since "people often refuse to relinquish their deep-seated beliefs even when presented with overwhelming evidence to contradict those beliefs."[15] The story of the track and field event known as the high jump is just one example.

Athletes competing in track and field jump over a horizontal bar for an event called the high jump. In the 19th century, athletes jumped over the bar using a straight-on approach or a scissoring of the legs technique as the jumper landed in sawdust landing pits. With advancements in the landing pads, jumpers started to implement the Western roll technique where the inner leg is used for the takeoff while the outer leg is thrust up to lead the body sideways over the bar.[16] While athletes worked on improving their performance, Portland, Oregon native Dick Fosbury eventually discovered a new technique during the 1960s that would revolutionize the event. Fosbury started jumping over bars in the fifth grade using the scissor-kick technique and cleared 3 feet 10 inches.

"In high school, despite the dire warnings of every coach who watched him, he invented the "Fosbury Flop" and reached 6 feet 7 inches. At the 1968 Mexico City Olympics, in front of 80,000 spectators, the 21-year-old Fosbury cleared a record-breaking 7 feet 41/4 inches."[17] After applying the Western roll technique for the early part of his career, Fosbury took advantage of the raised softer landing areas and leveraged such developments to think differently. As he approached the bar he directed himself over head and shoulders first, sliding over on his back and landing in a fashion that would likely have broken his neck in the old, sawdust landing pits. During Fosbury's early days of practicing his new technique at the University of Oregon, people said that his approach was unnecessary. The Usual Way of jumping over the bar was good enough. His approach went against the best practices of high jumping. Luckily Fosbury ignored those early critics and went on to establish a new way of thinking and jumping. Fosbury thought differently. Have you? Have you thought differently about your career lately? *Marketing Your Value* can help.

Many books offers advice on how to promote yourself, negotiate your salary, manage your career, create your brand, develop a résumé, or ace the interview. While these are important topics, there is a tremendous gap in the literature about marketing your value. This publication examines a variety of questions such as:

- What do you value?
- What do others value?
- Are you communicating your value for others to understand?
- What skills are valuable in today's challenging economy?
- Can you explain the value of your experiences in helping you go from who you were to who you are today?
- How much time do you set aside to figure out how your experiences and skills can help others with what they value?
- What types of employment positions allow you to demonstrate your value?
- If you have a job just for the money what can you do at night and on the weekend to live with purpose?

Navigating your career in today's dynamic and chaotic global marketplace demands that you present a clear, concise, and compelling message about your value. This publication walks you through the nine steps involved with the process divided into three sections: Assess, Brand, Communicate (ABC). The first section involves defining your life purpose, examining your relationship to success, and assessing your traits and habits. The second section involves building your brand by identifying your position, creating a plan of action, and maintaining a mindset to help manage the chaos. The final section involves communicating your value by designing impressive marketing materials, leveraging your network, and conducting an effective interview. Even the smallest step counts. Your busy life includes personal commitments, work, and whatever social life you have been able to carve out for yourself. Finding the time to complete the work outlined in this publication will require effort. Remember that everyone has the same amount of time that you do. Don't say you don't have enough time. You have exactly the same number of hours per day that were given to anyone who ever accomplished a goal, lived a life of purpose, or challenged the status quo. When you are pressed for time recall the words of Franz Kafka to his finance: "Time is short, my strength is limited, the office is a horror, the apartment is noisy, and if a pleasant, straightforward life is not possible, then one must try to wriggle through by subtle maneuvers."[18] Kafka worked at an insurance company while writing. He found a way to market his value, navigate his career, and live with purpose amidst the demands of a full-time job. So can you. I wish you well along your journey.

Michael Edmondson

The luckiest people are those who learn early that it's essential to take charge of your own life . . . you are the one who is responsible for you. No excuses. Don't blame others. Don't blame circumstances. You take charge. And one of the things you take charge of is your own learning. Life is an endless unfolding, and if we wish it to be, an endless process of self-discovery, and endless and unpredictable dialogue between our potentialities and the life situations in which we find ourselves.

John Gardner, Presidential Medal of Freedom recipient[19]

PART ONE

Assess

CHAPTER 1

Identify Your Purpose

Navigating your career requires you to identify your purpose. Failure to complete this step could keep you in a job with little or no meaning, stuck with no options, or paralyzed with fear to make even the slightest of change in your professional development. The search for meaning and authenticity is an essential human characteristic. Our work, our relationships, and our attitude shape our purpose. For our career to be purposeful we need to identify our authentic self. Career choice is not about the question "What can I do?" it's about the question "Who am I and who can I be?" As Viktor E. Frankl observed in *Man's Search for Meaning*, "Everyone has his own specific vocation or mission in life; everyone must carry out a concrete assignment that demands fulfillment. Everyone's task is unique as is his specific opportunity to implement it."[1]

All too often, however, obligations for work or family, global, political, and economic concerns or our personal health issues present barriers to living with intention and working with purpose. Our obligations require us to spend time, money, and resources. Global events involving politics and economics distract us. And the pursuit for personal health consumes our attention. These factors collide with increased frequency throughout our career and challenge our ability to navigate our career. But our age provides us with a greater source of knowledge and experience from which to define and redefine our purpose. The key is to not let these issues, or any others for that matter, distract us from achieving our destiny. Identifying your purpose and taking the first step to navigating your career involves the following exercises:

- Start with why
- The purpose audit

- The Greater Fool theory
- The milkshake exercise
- A.I.M. for your purpose

Start with Why

Instead of asking the question "What do I want to do with the rest of my life?" you should ask yourself "Why am I doing the work that I am doing?" This is a common question that often goes overlooked by individuals as they are caught up with just having a job so as to pay the bills. Would you like to have a career where the why matters more than just a paycheck? Many successful people and organizations reflect upon why they are doing what they are doing. In *Start with Why: How Great Leaders Inspire Everyone to Take Action*, Simon Sinek explains how *The Golden Circle* helps people understand why they do what they do. "It provides compelling evidence of how much more we can achieve if we remind ourselves to start everything we do by first asking why."[2]

To design The Golden Circle draw a small circle and write the word WHY in it, then draw a larger circle around that and write the word HOW in it, and finally draw a third circle around the other two and write the word WHAT in it. WHY is at the center of The Golden Circle. Sinek observed that all companies and people know what they do; some understand how they do what they do; but only a select few have examined why they do what they do. The Great Fire of London in 1666 provides an historical illustration in the value of asking why.

After the Great Fire, Sir Christopher Michael Wren, one of the most highly acclaimed English architects in history, had the responsibility for rebuilding 52 churches, including his masterpiece, St. Paul's Cathedral. The cathedral was built in a relative short time span: its first stone was laid on June 21, 1675, and the building was completed in 1711. Legend has it that Wren would often visit the construction site. During one of his visits Wren came across three stonecutters. Each was busy cutting a block of stone.

Interested in finding out what they were working on, he asked the first stonecutter what he was doing. "I am cutting a stone!" Still no wiser, Wren turned to the second stonecutter and asked him what he was doing.

"I am cutting this block of stone to make sure that it is square, and its dimensions are uniform, so that it will fit exactly in its place in a wall." A bit closer to finding out what the stonecutters were working on but still unclear, Wren turned to the third stonecutter. He seemed to be the happiest of the three and when asked what he was doing replied: "I am helping to build a great cathedral."[3]

Questions:

- The third stone mason clearly understood why he was doing what he was doing. Do you?

- When is the last time you thought about why you were doing what you were doing?

- If Wren asked you the same question he asked the stone masons, how would you answer?

- Do you work for an organization that understands why it does what it does?

The Purpose Audit

Throughout this workbook there will be audits for you to complete. An audit asks numerous questions on a specific topic. The intent is for you to engage in reflection long enough to heighten your self-awareness. A higher level of self-awareness provides a strong foundation for the other aspects involved with navigating your career. This audit challenges you to consider 10 statements and corresponding questions related to the level that you currently live and work with purpose.

1. **How often do you practice being present?** In a given day how often are you fully present and think about what it is you are doing to be an engaged participant? When you are figuring out your life purpose, realize that what you are also doing is being present. As Eckhart Tolle observed, "The more you are focused on time—past and future—the more you miss the Now, the most precious thing there is."[4]

a. How much time in a given day do you spend thinking about the past or the future?

b. If you were to assign percentages to your day per section, what would your answer be? (e.g., 20 percent of my day I dwell on the past; 60 percent of my day I worry about the future. For 20 percent of the day I find myself fully present.)

    i. _____ of my day is spent with me dwelling on the past.

    ii. _____ of my day is spent distracted about the future.

    iii. _____ of my day is when I am fully present in the Now.

2. **You learn how to manage fear.** Figuring out your life purpose usually involves some degree of courage to manage your fear. All too often, however, people choose not to follow a career path because of the fear of the unknown, fear of failure, or perhaps even fear of success. Once you learn how to manage fear you can more easily navigate your career and work with purpose instead of just having a job you dislike. Mark Twain once noted that the definition of courage "is resistance to fear, mastery of fear, not absence of fear."

a. Are you afraid of failure? If so, why?

b. If you have ever failed, what lessons did you learn?

c. What is currently holding you back from navigating your career?

3. **You recognize that progress is small.** Living with purpose and navigating your career with intention means recognizing that progress will indeed be small on most days. With that in mind, it is important to remember the words of American artist Jasper Johns: "Do something, do something to that, and then do something to that. Pretty soon you have something."[5] "Pretty soon" may be a few years, or even more, but the point is you kept going and made small progress whenever and wherever possible.

a. Do you get overwhelmed with the larger issues in life or are you able to break them down into small components?

b. Are you comfortable completing one small task after another for an extended period of time to complete a large project?

c. Have you ever quit something you started? Why do you think that happened?

4. **You understand that anything is possible.** Those who live with purpose usually encounter one issue after another. They stay determined

and figure out a way to address each situation by understanding that anything is possible. As Laurence Gonzales concluded in his study *Deep Survival: Why Lives, Who Dies and Why*, "they believe anything is possible and act accordingly."[6]

a. Do you believe that anything is possible?

b. If not, what is holding you back from that belief?

c. How often do you find yourself creating options for your life?

5. **You get to kick your own ass.** There will probably come a time in the pursuit of your purpose that you will need a kick in the pants. At that point you will need to recall the words of motivational speaker Eric Thomas, "When you want to succeed as bad as you want to breathe, then you'll be successful."[7]

a. Just how badly do you want to navigate your career and live with purpose?

b. Do you want it succeed as you want to take your next breath?

c. How much energy and time have you devoted to living a life of purpose?

d. Have you convinced yourself that living a life of purpose is out of reach?

6. **You break up the routine.** Navigating your career and living with purpose will challenge you to break up the established routine so you can continue on an unexplored path. Author Paulo Coelho made a blunt observation about routines when he wrote, "To those who believe that adventures are dangerous, I say, try routine; that kills you far more quickly."[8] While certain routines may help improve your time management, you need to assess if it has had a negative impact on your ability to navigate the next step of your career.

a. Are you so comfortable in your routine that you have stopped looking for the next step along your career path?

b. Are you sacrificing a life of purpose to maintain a secure routine?

c. How do you know if your routine is prohibiting you from exploring options?

7. **You work on your listening skills.** You will undoubtedly need the assistance of others as you look to translate your purpose from vision into reality. Listening to what others have to offer is a prerequisite

for navigating your career. With that in mind, remember what Diogenes Laërtius, biographer of the Greek philosophers, said "We have two ears and only one tongue in order that we may hear more and speak less."

a. Are you listening twice as much as you are speaking?

b. When is the last time you assessed how much listening you engage in on a given day?

c. How often do you work on your listening skills?

8. **You find perspective in life.** Finding perspective and looking at the big picture will help you live with purpose. Living with purpose allows you opportunities to challenge your perspective on life. The key is to keep an open mind so that you can search for different perspectives that can help you move forward as you translate your purpose into action.

a. How frequently do you change your perspective in life?

b. Do you actively seek out how others view the world?

c. Do you maintain the self-awareness to realize that your perspective requires a change?

9. **You focus on your efforts.** It is almost impossible to live with purpose without being focused for extended periods of time. You need to cut down on the distractions in your life, as Gaylon Ferguson, in the book *Natural Wakefulness* said that "Distraction is married to discontent."[9] The longer you are distracted the less focus you will have in learning how to market your value.

a. How easily distracted from your life purpose are you?

b. Have you ever been distracted while navigating your career? If so, what happened?

c. Did you assess your level of discontent while being distracted?

d. Are you using your distraction as an excuse not to pursue your life purpose?

10. **You are humbled.** As you make progress toward your purpose, remind yourself to stay humbled along the way. Ernest Hemingway noted that "there is nothing noble in being superior to your fellow man; true nobility is being superior to your former self." When you live with purpose you focus on yourself and understand that humility is a key component of personal growth.

Questions:

a. Do you actively practice humility?

b. Are you working hard at being superior to your former self?

c. How much time do you spend comparing yourself to others?

The Greater Fool Theory

The greater fool theory (also called survivor investing) is the belief held by one who makes a questionable investment, with the assumption that they will be able to sell it later to "a greater fool." This form of investing rests upon the foundation that a buyer believes he can sell the stock at a higher price than purchased. When applied to fields outside of economics, the term greater fool means someone who combines self-delusion with ego so as to succeed where others have failed. In the final episode of *The Newsroom* (Season 1, 2013), the term "greater fool" was used to describe the show's main character, Will McAvoy (Jeff Daniels), because of his belief in doing "real news." Throughout the episode, Will views it as a negative term. However, financial reporter Sloan Sabbith (Olivia Munn) tells Will, "The greater fool is someone with the perfect blend of self-delusion and ego to think that he can succeed where others have failed. This whole country was made by greater fools."[10]

One example of a greater fool is the Chick-fil-A founder S. Truett Cathy. Cathy challenged the status quo when he opened his first Chick-fil-A store in Atlanta's Greenbriar Mall in 1967. True to his Christian business practices, Cathy told mall management that his store had to be closed on Sunday. Since he launched his other restaurant, The Dwarf Grill, in 1946, Truett had never been open on Sunday and wanted to continue the tradition. Amidst protests from the mall management that told him Sunday would be his busiest day Cathy challenged the status quo and stayed true to his principles. "He believed that all franchised Chick-fil-A Operators and their Restaurant employees should have an opportunity to rest, spend time with family and friends, and worship if they choose to do so."[11] This greater fool passed away at the age of 93 in September 2014 and was described by former President Jimmy Carter "as a blessing to countless people."[12]

Questions:

- Do you have any interest in being a greater fool? Why? Why not?
- Do you know of any greater fools?
- What personal traits and habits does a greater fool need to practice?
- What is the relationship between being a greater fool and living with purpose?

The Milkshake Exercise

In *How Will You Measure Your Life*, Clayton Christensen shares the story of a fast-food restaurant chain that hired his research company to understand why 40 percent of milkshakes were purchased in the morning. Interviews with customers who purchased a morning milkshake revealed that they had a long commute to work. The milkshake was easy to drink in the car, filled them until lunch, and was enjoyable to drink. The researchers concluded that customers hired the milkshake to do a very specific job. The customers faced a long, boring commute, had one free hand, and needed something to stave off hunger until noon. The milkshake was hired in lieu of a bagel or doughnut because it was relatively tidy and appetite-quenching, and because trying to suck a thick liquid through a thin straw gave customers something to do with their boring commute. To improve customer satisfaction, the "company created a morning milkshake that was even thicker (to last through a long commute) and more interesting (with chunks of fruit) than its predecessor."[13] The chain also created a different milkshake more appealing to parents who wanted to provide a special treat for their children. This milkshake, unlike the morning version, was easier for young children to drink.[14] When marketing your value to others, learn to apply lessons from the milkshake story and ask others what specific tasks they need completed. Doing so can help you figure out if what they have available is a good fit with your skill set and purpose.

Questions:

- What lessons can you take away from the milkshake story and how can you apply them to your life?

- When have you hired someone to be your milkshake and fill a specific need? In other words, do you have people you talk to when specific situations or questions arise in your life?

- When do people hire you to be their milkshake? In other words, why do certain people come and talk to you? Increase your self-awareness and work hard at recognizing who comes to you, why they do so, and what you have to offer them.

A.I.M. for Your Purpose

Obligations via work or family, global political and economic concerns, and our personal health are three significant issues to living with intention and working with purpose. Our obligations require us to spend time, money, and resources. Global events involving politics and economics distract us. And the pursuit for personal health consumes our attention. As we age, these factors collide with increased frequency and challenge our ability to live with intention and work with purpose. But our age provides us with a greater source of knowledge and experience from which to define and redefine our purpose. The key is to not let these three issues, or any others for that matter, distract us from achieving our destiny. As William Jennings Bryan once wrote, "Destiny is not a matter of chance; it is a matter of choice. It is not a thing to be waited for; it is a thing to be achieved." So how exactly can you identify your destiny or purpose amidst the convergence of issues? How can one determine a way to life with intention and work with purpose while simultaneously fulfilling their obligations? It is possible. If you make defining your purpose a priority all you have to do is complete a simple three step exercise called "A.I.M. for Your Purpose:"

To complete this exercise you will need to answer three questions using the A.I.M. acronym for (Action, Individual, and Mission). If you wish to have more than one purpose, and most people are capable of doing so, then complete this exercise by answering three questions:

- What **A**ction do you want to take?
- What **I**ndividuals do you want to help?
- What **M**ission do you want to accomplish?

Below are two examples:

- Purpose #1: I want to teach (action) undergraduates (individuals) that they have more career options than they realize (mission).
- Purpose #2: I want to help (action) small business owners (individuals) understand that their small business will only grow as much as they grow personally (mission).

Once completed post this exercise somewhere you will see it each day. As you develop both personally and professionally, challenge yourself to update your purpose. After all, you just need to A.I.M.!

CHAPTER 2

Explore Your Relationship to Success

After you identify your purpose, the second step to navigating your career involves exploring your relationship to success. Doing so allows you to be open to a variety of career opportunities. If your definition of success includes only one type of job, does that really maximize your opportunity to succeed? Knowing how you define success will also help you manage your energy. In today's chaotic global marketplace you will need to rely on your energy quite often so as to adapt to challenges. Common definitions of success often involve the achievement of financial wealth, the accumulation of luxurious consumer goods, the acquisition of housing estates, and the collection of high-performance automobiles. Current research indicates three emerging trends. First, there here has been a "substantial decrease in the number of people who believe money is the only real meaningful measure of success."[1] Second, the number of Americans who associate success with life experiences over the purchase of consumer goods continues to grow.[2] Moreover, during the last 30 years Americans increasingly viewed life satisfaction, such as good health, finding time for loved ones, and creating a work–life balance as all signs of success."[3] How do you define success? This chapter provides four exercises to help you answer that question:

- The Elements of Success Audit
- Your Choice to Pursue Success
- Growth Mindset Questions
- Growth Mindset Quiz

The Elements of Success

The 2013 *American Express Life Twist* study identified 10 elements of success commonly expressed by Americans:[4]

- Good health
- Finding time for the important things in life
- Having a good marriage/relationship
- Knowing how to spend money well
- Having a good work/personal life balance
- Having a job I love
- Making the time to pursue your passions and interests
- Being physically fit
- Embracing new experiences/changes
- Always trying to learn and do new things

How would you rank order these 10 elements?

Example: In this example the respondent placed work/personal life balance at the top because he/she defines success as being physically fit and maintaining good health. This professional is well aware that an imbalance between one's work/personal lives can create both physical and mental stress, so he/she has consciously made a decision to place these three elements at the top of her life.

1. Having a good work/personal life balance
2. Being physically fit
3. Good health
4. Knowing how to spend money well
5. Finding time for the important things in life
6. Making the time to pursue your passions and interests
7. Embracing new experiences/changes
8. Always trying to learn and do new things
9. Having a job I love
10. Having a good marriage/relationship

The Elements of Success Audit

How would you rank order (from most important to least important) the 10 elements of success?

1. _____
2. _____
3. _____
4. _____
5. _____
6. _____
7. _____
8. _____
9. _____
10. _____

Questions:

- Why did you place these elements in this order?
- Have these changed over time for you?

Defining the Success of Others

Now that you have rank ordered the elements of your success, circle three of the following elements of success you feel define the success of others. Another way of thinking about this is when you are thinking about a friend, family member, or reviewing the credentials of someone you are interviewing, which of the following three elements are most important to you when deciding if they have been successful?

- Happiness levels
- Family life
- Life experiences
- How much money they make

- How generous they are to others
- How educated they are
- The nature of their job
- How physically fit/healthy they are
- Their involvement in volunteer/community events
- How they present themselves on social media (e.g., Facebook)

Why did you choose these elements? Have you noticed that you judge the success of others on these elements?

Your Choice to Pursue Success

Life satisfaction is now an important sign of success for many people. But what is truly astonishing is the realization that for the first time in history "it matters not so much where you are born or what your DNA says about you – today's global economy is waiting for you to step forward, with only the resistance to hold you back."[5] But will you choose to pursue success? Will you choose to navigate your career to live with purpose? The book publishing industry is a perfect example of what happens when people step up and navigate their career to live with purpose and choose to do something they have always wanted to do—write a book. Self-published books now represent 31 percent of e-book sales on Amazon's Kindle Store, and independent authors are taking "significant market share in all genres."[6] Self-published authors have decided to pursue success. Have you?

Questions:

- Will you step forward and translate your dream into reality?
- Will you take the necessary time to understand how to be successful?
- Will you recognize the tremendous potential that today's technology driven global marketplace offers?
- Will you take responsibility for your career and take a more active role in navigating your career?
- If you decided to pursue success and failed what did you then do?

Growth Mindset

The Irish playwright George Bernard Shaw once observed, "People are always blaming their circumstances for what they are. I do not believe in circumstances. The people who get on in this world are the people who get up and look for the circumstances that they want, and if they can't find them, make them." While Shaw has a point, it might be more exact to say that "the people who get on in this world" have a growth mindset. In her 2006 publication, *Mindset: The New Psychology of Success*, Carol Dweck concluded that people have either "fixed" or "growth" mindsets.[7]

Those with a fixed mindset believe that "they are the way they are." This mindset believes that one's level of athleticism and mathematical capacities are fixed and have little room for improvement. Believing they are born with a certain amount of talent, fixed mindset individuals seldom challenge their abilities due to the possibility of failure. Fixed mindset individuals see improvement as a zero-sum game where there is a chance of failure. Those with a growth mindset, however, believe that they can improve by exercising their brain through hard work and practicing skills like athleticism. Growth mindset individuals have a desire to improve and view such development, even with its risk of failure, as a positive-sum game. This dedication to improvement drives growth mindset individuals forward despite great odds.

Questions:

- Do you have a fixed or growth mindset? How do you know?
- Do you know anyone with a fixed mindset?
- Do you know anyone with a growth mindset?

Growth Mindset Quiz

Directions: This quiz tests your awareness of the differences between growth and fixed mindsets. For each of the following statements write down whether it belongs to a fixed or growth mindset. Answers are on the following page. For example: "Intelligence is something people are born with that can't be changed." Does that statement belong to someone who a growth or fixed mindset?

1. Intelligence is something people are born with that can't be changed.

2. No matter how intelligent you are, you can always be more intelligent.

3. You can always substantially change how intelligent you are.

4. You are a certain kind of person, and there is not much that can be done to really change that.

5. You can always change basic things about the kind of person you are.

6. Musical talent can be learned by anyone.

7. Only a few people will be truly good at sports, you have to be "born with it."

8. Math is much easier to learn if you are male or may be come from a culture who values math.

9. The harder you work at something, the better you will beat it.

10. No matter what kind of person you are, you can always change substantially.

11. Trying new things is stressful for me and I avoid it.

12. Some people are good and kind and some are not; it's not often that people change.

13. I appreciate when people, parents, coaches, and teachers give me feedback about my performance.

14. I often get angry when I get negative feedback about my performance.

15. All human beings are capable of learning.

16. You can learn new things, but you can't really change how intelligent you are.

17. You can do things differently, but the important parts of who you are can't really be changed.

18. Human beings are basically good, but sometimes make terrible decisions.

19. An important reason why I do my school work is that I like to learn new things.

20. Truly smart people do not need to try hard.

Questions:

- What three or five statements above do you agree with? Why is that?
- Can you demonstrate examples from your life for two or more of the statements?
- Have you seen others exemplify one or more of these statements?

Answers to Growth Mindset Quiz

1. Intelligence is something people are born with that can't be changed. FIXED
2. No matter how intelligent you are, you can always be more intelligent. GROWTH
3. You can always substantially change how intelligent you are. GROWTH
4. You are a certain kind of person, and there is not much that can be done to really change that. FIXED
5. You can always change basic things about the kind of person you are. GROWTH
6. Musical talent can be learned by anyone. GROWTH
7. Only a few people will be truly good at sports, you have to be "born with it." FIXED
8. Math is much easier to learn if you are male or may be come from a culture who values math. FIXED
9. The harder you work at something, the better you will beat it. GROWTH
10. No matter what kind of person you are, you can always change substantially. GROWTH
11. Trying new things is stressful for me and I avoid it. FIXED
12. Some people are good and kind and some are not; it's not often that people change. FIXED
13. I appreciate when people, parents, coaches, and teachers give me feedback about my performance. GROWTH
14. I often get angry when I get negative feedback about my performance. FIXED

15. All human beings are capable of learning. GROWTH
16. You can learn new things, but you can't really change how intelligent you are. FIXED
17. You can do things differently, but the important parts of who you are can't really be changed. FIXED
18. Human beings are basically good, but sometimes make terrible decisions. GROWTH
19. An important reason why I do my school work is that I like to learn new things. GROWTH
20. Truly smart people do not need to try hard. FIXED

CHAPTER 3

Assess Your Skills and Traits

Now that you have identified your purpose in step one and explored your relationship to success in step two, you can begin the process of assessing your skills and traits in step three. Access to overwhelming amounts of information anywhere, anytime, on any device is a central hallmark of our time. Therefore, "What you know matters far less than what you can do with what you know. The ability to solve problems creatively—and skills like critical thinking, communication, and collaboration are far more important" than your ability to memorize large amounts of information.[1] All too often people are worried about what they know instead of how they process the acquisition of information and then apply that to solve a problem, ask more questions, or network with people to share what they have learned. Assessing your skills and traits can offer the much needed insight into your behavior and help you understand how you use what you know to market your value, live with purpose, and navigate your career. This step requires you to complete the following exercises:

- The Traits and Habits of Success People
- Your Personal Assessment of the Traits and Habits (PATH) to Success
- Distractions
- Professional Skills Audit

The Traits and Habits of Successful People

The ability to engage in routine self-evaluations of personal traits and professional skills is a necessary component of communicating one's value to the marketplace. The Personal Assessment of Traits and Habits (PATH) to Success lists 20 of the most common personal traits and habits frequently practiced by successful professionals and organizations. The broadest definition of success is used here. The examples included in each of the 20 traits and habits transcend industries, backgrounds, and cultures. My research illustrates very clearly that there are additional traits and habits, so I only included the top 20 here. While successful professionals also exhibit other traits, these 20 represent a solid foundation for individuals dedicated to achieving the personal growth required to develop professional skills. Additionally, not every successful person practices each trait or habit all of the time.

I use the word practice with PATH instead of strengths and weaknesses because PATH is a practice and not a muscle group. Individuals need to practice PATH on a regular basis so as to think more effectively, take action, and achieve the personal growth required to market their value and navigate their career. By defining the frequency of how often a trait or habit is used, one leaves the door open for making even the smallest of steps in a daily practice of traveling further down their PATH. Remember if you have never done something or rarely do it, it is not a weakness; it's just that you have yet to practice that trait or habit with any frequency. As Jason Fried and David Heinemeier Hansson noted in their best-selling book *Rework*:

> You know those overnight-success stories you've heard about? It's not the whole story. Dig deeper and you'll usually find people who have busted their asses for years to get into a position where things could take off . . . Trade the dream of overnight success for slow, measured growth. It's hard, but you have to be patient. You have to grind it out. You have to do it for a long time before the right people notice.[2]

Here are the 20 traits and habits you can consider practicing "for a long time before the right people notice."

1. <u>Believe you create your own life</u>: The influence of other people and circumstances are all around us, but you need to believe that you can make an impact on them if you want to achieve your goals. Believing you create your own life helps you understand that you alone are responsible for your beliefs. What you believe will help you travel the

path from being the person you are to becoming the person you want to be. Madame Walker believed she created her own life. Regarded as the first female African–American self-made millionaire, Walker was an American entrepreneur who rose from extreme hardship to develop a successful line of beauty and hair products for women.[3]

2. Create a vision for your life: Having an idea as to where to go, where you need to turn, and what resources you need along the way are the three design elements required to create a vision for your life. Your vision can be multidimensional with different paths to travel and can also change throughout your life. If you have no vision, however, it will be difficult to move forward since you will have no idea where to go. Jack Dorsey has a vision for his life. As the founder and CEO of Twitter and Square, Dorsey is an American web developer and businessman who recently stated that his vision is to be the Mayor of New York City one day.[4]

3. Define a specific goal: It is impossible to work toward something if you do not know exactly what it is you are trying to achieve. Charles Kemmons Wilson defined a specific goal of creating the Holiday Inn chain of hotels that were friendly to families. Wilson came up with the idea after a family road trip during which he was disappointed by the quality provided by motels of that era.[5]

4. Exercise self-discipline: Once you have clearly identified a vision and goals, it requires inner drive and deliberate effort over an extended period of time to achieve them. Exercising self-discipline is extremely important to accomplish almost anything in life. "You may not have connections, or an education, or wealth, but with enough passion and seat, you can make anything happen."[6] Christopher Paul Gardner used this attitude and exercised self-discipline to overcome homelessness to become an American entrepreneur, investor, stockbroker, motivational speaker, author, and philanthropist.[7]

5. Deal with change: The world is in constant motion and people that live with intention and work with purpose have to deal with change on a constant basis. Instead of avoiding or ignoring change, it is important to recognize its existence and figure out ways to manage the change to live life with intention and work with purpose. Gabrielle "Coco" Bonheur Chanel dealt with change as she had to

overcome a difficult childhood and became a French fashion designer and founder of the Chanel brand. She was the only fashion designer to appear on *Time* magazine's list of the 100 most influential people of the 20th century.[8]

6. Rebound from failure: Nobody is successful all the time with everything they try to do. If we give up after a failure or two we will fall short of achieving the life we envision. Few, if any, people or organizations achieved success without experiencing some degree of failure along the way. Eric Thomas rebounded from failure as a high school dropout to eventually obtain his graduate degree and developed The Advantage Program, an undergraduate retention program targeting academically high-risk students of color.[9]

7. Believe in yourself when others do not: Your goals and desires are uniquely yours and may not be shared by anyone else. To achieve them you must retain self-confidence in what you are doing despite what others say. Despite predictions that they would never succeed, Orville & Wilbur Wright believed in each other and pioneered aviation by becoming the first to successfully power and sustain heavier-than-air human flight, on December 17, 1903.[10]

8. Exhibit courageous behavior: Courage is facing situations that scare us but demand our attention if we want to take action and achieve a new goal. Valentino Deng demonstrated courageous behavior by building schools in Sudan, the very place where decades earlier the Second Sudanese Civil War wiped out his village. Deng is one of the Lost Boys of Sudan— the name given to 20,000 boys who were displaced and/or orphaned during the Second Sudanese Civil War (1983–2005).[11]

9. Get comfortable being uncomfortable: Many things in life make us uncomfortable so we must routinely practice getting comfortable in uncomfortable situations, both personally and professionally. Doing so can help us take the smallest of steps toward our next goal. Dick Fosbury was able to get comfortable being uncomfortable and revolutionized the high jump event, inventing a unique "back-first" technique, now known as the Fosbury Flop, adopted by almost all high jumpers today. His method was to sprint diagonally toward the bar, then curve and leap backward over the bar.[12]

10. <u>Persevere through a difficult situation</u>: Reaching any goal requires you to keep moving forward no matter what the obstacle or how difficult the situation. Mario Renato Capecchi persevered through a difficult situation when as a child he was left to fend for himself on the streets of northern Italy for 4 years, living in various orphanages; he almost died of malnutrition. After being reunited with his mother, they moved to the United States and Capecchi eventually became a molecular geneticist and a cowinner of the 2007 Nobel Prize in Physiology or Medicine.[13]

11. <u>Be more resourceful</u>: Be aware that other resources or people might exist to help you answer a question, address an issue, or resolve a problem. Crowdsourcing, collaboration tools, and social media sites are just three of the categories of new resources that have emerged during the last decade. Jimmy Wales learned to be more resourceful when he helped create Wikipedia after two previous business ventures provided the funding he needed to launch the free online encyclopedia.[14]

12. <u>Prioritize your to-do list</u>: There are many things we have to do, but not all things are necessary for us to meet our timelines and accomplish our goals. Fred Smith prioritized his to-do list to become the founder, chairman, president, and CEO of FedEx, originally known as Federal Express, the first overnight express delivery company in the world.[15]

13. <u>Collaborate with others</u>: Working with others can make you more effective by exponentially increasing your capabilities. Being a part of a team made up of people from different cultures, generations, and functional areas is expected of today's employees. The more you can practice collaboration the better off you will be in the workplace. Paul Orfalea collaborated with others when he grew his first Kinko's store in 1970 to a network of over 80 stores in the U.S. Rather than franchise, Orfalea formed partnerships with each individual store's local co-owners.[16]

14. <u>Differentiate yourself</u>: Examine your traits and skills so you can identify what makes you unique and valuable to others in a specific situation. S. Truett Cathy differentiated himself when he launched Chick-fil-A restaurant chain centered on the chicken sandwich.

A devout Baptist, Truett further differentiated himself by always closing his stores on Sunday.[17]

15. Communicate your value: Present a compelling story about yourself so that others can better understand how you differentiate and offer value to them. Sheryl Sandberg, author of *Lean In: Women, Work, and the Will to Lead*, urges women to communicate their value to advocate for themselves whether in the workplace, home, or in school. As Sandberg notes, "women only hold around 14% of Fortune 500 executive officer positions and about 17% of board seats" and therefore need to lean in and communicate their value and have their voices heard.[18]

16. Understand events and people more clearly: Assumptions block communication, hurt collaboration, and derail action. As a world-renowned glass sculptor, Dale Chihuly needed to understand events and people more clearly when glass blinded him in a car accident. Unable to create the glass art he taught others how to blow glass and learned how to become "more choreographer than dancer, more supervisor than participant, more director than actor."[19]

17. Respect and discuss new ideas: Growth comes from inviting, processing, and implementing new ideas without judging the validity of those ideas before thinking about them. New perspectives can help you become more creative and open opportunities. Remember, "the world is complex and uncertain; our understanding of it is incomplete."[20] One person who respects and discusses new ideas is Associate Professor of Cultural Anthropology at Kansas State University, Michael Wesch. Through speeches and well-received YouTube videos, Wesch has explained new ideas, especially the effect of new media on human interaction through the emerging field of digital ethnography.[21]

18. Take calculated risks: To live with intention is to move forward without a guaranteed outcome because one or more of the variables are unknown. Philip Petite was a French high-wire artist who took a calculated risk and gained fame for his high-wire walk between the Twin Towers of the World Trade Center in New York City, New York, on August 7, 1974. As he mentioned in the award-winning document *Man on Wire*: "Life should be lived on the edge of life.

You have to exercise rebellion: to refuse to tape yourself to rules, to refuse your own success, to refuse to repeat yourself, to see every day, every year, every idea as a true challenge—and then you are going to live your life on a tightrope."[22]

19. Ask yourself empowering questions: Question what is happening around you to deepen your understanding. Instead of lamenting when something occurs, you can ask "what is life trying to teach me at this very moment?" Randy Pausch was an American professor of computer science at Carnegie Mellon University. Upon learning that he had pancreatic cancer in September 2006, he asked himself empowering questions and gave an upbeat lecture titled "The Last Lecture: Really Achieving Your Childhood Dreams" on September 18, 2007. Pausch died of complications from pancreatic cancer on July 25, 2008.[23]

20. Practice self-improvement: The more you intentionally improve the other traits and habits the more effective you become in other areas of your life. Only you can take the steps needed to practice self-improvement on a regular basis as you look to achieve the personal growth required for professional development. Reid Hoffman is an American entrepreneur, venture capitalist, and author who cofounded LinkedIn. In his book *The Start-Up of You*, Hoffman wrote that we are all in a state of permanent beta. "Each day presents an opportunity to learn more, do more, grow more. Permanent beta is a lifelong commitment to continuous personal growth."[24]

Your Personal Assessment of the Traits and Habits (PATH) to Success

Directions: Now that you have reviewed each of the 20 traits and habits of successful people, use the Likert scale: **Never • Rarely • Sometimes• Most of the Time • Always** to determine how frequently you practiced each trait and habit. Additionally, select a specific period of time such as a month or a week. Doing so allows you to focus on your frequency of practice for each trait and habit during a small window of time. Also be sure to write down today's date and then periodically complete this audit to track your progress over time.

<u>Example</u>: During the last month I sometimes practiced the trait of believing that I create my own life.

Today's date: _____

1. **Believe you create your own life.** _____
2. **Create a vision for your life.** _____
3. **Define a specific goal.** _____
4. **Exercise self-discipline.** _____
5. **Deal with change.** _____
6. **Rebound from failure.** _____
7. **Believe in yourself when others do.** _____
8. **Exhibit courage.** _____
9. **Get comfortable being uncomfortable.** _____
10. **Persevere through a difficult situation.** _____
11. **Be more resourceful.** _____
12. **Prioritize your to-do list.** _____
13. **Collaborate with others.** _____
14. **Differentiate yourself.** _____
15. **Communicate your value.** _____
16. **Understand events and people more.** _____
17. **Respect and discuss new ideas.** _____
18. **Take calculated risks.** _____
19. **Ask yourself empowering questions.** _____
20. **Practice self-improvement.** _____

<u>Next Steps and Goals</u>: Identify one or two traits and habits you would like to work on during a given period of time and keep track of your progress. For example, "On Monday night between 7:30 and 8:00 p.m., I am going to work on discussing and understanding new issues and their implications for the future by reading a *New York Times* editorial. My goal is to do this every Monday for the next 4 weeks."

Questions:

- What one or two traits and habits have you identified to practice with more frequency?

- Why did you choose those traits and habits?
- What specifically will you do to practice each one?

Distractions

Marketing your value and navigating your career require substantial investments of time. The more distracted you are the less likely you are to live a life of purpose. How well do you manage your time? Are you leveraging time well-enough that you are able to place a priority on marketing your value? Generally speaking, there are two types of time: physical and cerebral. Physical is easy to understand as there are only 24 hours in a day. Remember this one hard fact: everyone has the same amount of time in a day. 24 hours is all anyone is given. What people do with their time varies, but not the amount of it. And as author H. Jackson Brown Jr. reminded us: "Don't say you don't have enough time. You have exactly the same number of hours per day that were given to Helen Keller, Pasteur, Michelangelo, Mother Teresa, Leonardo da Vinci, Thomas Jefferson, and Albert Einstein."[25] How you spend your physical time tells a lot about how you view life, what you value, and also illustrates your level of commitment to your goals. Navigating your career will require time.

The other type of time is cerebral that involves what people spend their very limited physical time thinking about or focused on. Cerebral time occurs in your mind and consists of the various distractions that prohibit people from living a life of intention and working with purpose. Some distractions are indeed healthy and serve as a moment of much needed cerebral or physical rest. Many distractions, however, are time-consuming. Sporting events, concerts, and lives of celebrities are common distractions. One example of just how preoccupied people are comes in a study of news sources that found out that Americans "viewed twelve times as many pages about Miley Cyrus as they did about the war in Syria even though the news sources published 2.4 Syria articles for every one about Miley."[26] Despite more than twice the news coverage on the war in Syria, people were obsessed with finding out about Miley Cyrus. Is that the best way to use your limited time alive? All too often people misuse their time and then wake up years later only to find out they are unable to market their value, navigate their career, or live with purpose. So that you do not make the same mistakes, here are the 15 most time-consuming distractions to recognize:

1. Preoccupation with others
2. Fixation with athletes
3. Fascination with actors
4. Adoration of musicians
5. Pontification of lifestyle
6. Addiction to political issues
7. Obsession with social media
8. Addiction to television
9. Apprehension about the past
10. Trepidation for the future
11. Occupation with technology
12. Infatuation with your body
13. Consumption of Information
14. Anxiety about money
15. Fear of loving or losing love

Distraction Audit

Directions: Answer the following questions to better understand just how distractions impact your physical and cerebral time.

1. What percentage of time in a given day do you find yourself preoccupied with one or more of these distractions?
2. Has this preoccupation had a negative impact on your mental or physical health?
3. Have you allowed the distraction to stop you in the pursuit of a goal?
4. Has a distraction had a negative impact on your financial situation?
5. How much time do you allow any one person/s inside your head? What is it about that person that preoccupies your time and thoughts?
6. Sports and games are fun and relaxing. But do you need to watch every single game on television or go to every home game? How much money are you spending on going to or watching games?

7. Do you follow your favorite musicians all around the country? Exactly how much time and money does the adoration of musicians cost you? Do you place a musician (or athlete or actor) on a pedestal almost as if to worship them? Why is this so?

8. Do you only eat certain foods, shop at certain stores, or drink certain tea? Must you tell every single person you meet your lifestyle choices regarding food, the environment, or some other issue?

9. Are you so staunchly held to one political party that you are unable to consider new ideas?

10. The advent of social media has created entirely new distractions. How much time do you spend on social media sites?

11. Television shows certainly provide a much needed distraction but are you addicted to a television show? Do you feel as though you are part of the cast?

12. By definition the past already happened. It's over. With that in mind, ask yourself how much time you spend worrying about that which has already happened?

13. The beautiful thing about tomorrow is that it never arrives. There is only today and this moment. Are you so scared about the future that your fear has distracted you from living in the present?

14. Mobile phone, tablets, and lap tops have greatly enhanced our connectivity to one another. But must you have the latest version of a device?

15. Staying healthy through diet, exercise, and rest is important but are you infatuated with your body? Do you obsess over how you look all the time?

16. In today's age of information overload it is very easy to be distracted by information. Must you read every new book, article, and blog post?

17. Can you take your time with love or do you rush into it? Or perhaps are you so distracted by the loss of love you won't allow yourself to love in the first place?

Remember, some distractions are indeed fine and even necessary. Only you can determine if the distractions actually prohibit you from living with intention and working with purpose. If, however, you remain unhappy, unfulfilled, or unsatisfied with some aspect of your life, perhaps it is time to think differently. Perhaps it is time to divert your attention from that which is prohibiting you from translating your vision into reality.

Professional Skills

Now that you have assessed your personal traits and habits it is necessary to assess your professional skills. If it is true that individuals rely on different traits and habits to succeed personally, it is equally true that professionals rely on different skills to succeed in the workplace. Much like the 20 traits and habits of successful people, however, being a 21st century professional does require a certain demonstrate of key skills. A lifelong commitment to development, each of these professional skills is a prerequisite for marketing your value and navigating your career in today's chaotic and hypercompetitive global marketplace. Unfortunately, the vast majority of college students and experienced individuals spend far too little time identifying, assessing, and developing their professional skills. Over 70 percent of employers said recent college graduates lack communication, creativity, collaboration, and critical thinking skills they need to work today's jobs."[27]

No matter your industry, position, or background, all working individuals and professionals need a lifelong commitment to developing their professional skills. This is especially true for individuals with 15 or more years of experience. In today's challenging environment employers are leaving positions unfilled because they are unable to identify qualified candidates. It's no surprise then one survey found that "one-third of 848 small business owners and chief executives said they had unfilled job openings in June 2014 because they couldn't identify qualified applicants."[28] Don't assume that just because a position is open that the employer will fill it. Employers will routinely leave a position unfilled if they are unable to find a qualified candidate who fits into the organizational culture.

Listed below are the top 15 professional skills employers across all industries need their employers to demonstrate to remain competitive today. Examples of how you would demonstrate each skill are listed below each one.

1. Being flexible while managing multiple tasks.
   a. Demonstrates an ability to achieve desired results.
   b. Delivers reliable and sustained results while effectively dealing with issues as they arise during the process.
   c. Delegates to improve organizational effectiveness.

2. Collaborating with others or working as a team member.
   a. Inspires cooperation and confidence.
   b. Promotes cooperative behavior and team efforts.
   c. Gives careful consideration to tactical alternatives.
   d. Recognizes value of others, regardless of position or experience.
3. Communicating by listening, writing, or speaking.
   a. Makes effective and proper use of communication platforms and devices.
   b. Is able to communicate complex information into user-friendly terms.
   c. Encourages honest feedback.
   d. Schedules meetings only when absolutely necessary.
4. Completing assignments independently.
   a. Meets responsibilities promptly.
   b. Achieves results when confronted with major responsibilities and limited resources.
   c. Comfortable asking questions to ensure deliverable is completed as designed.
5. Connecting choices and actions to ethical decisions.
   a. Maintains high personal integrity.
   b. Adheres to ethical principles that reflect the highest standards of organizational and individual behavior.
   c. Is regarded as highly trustful, sincere, and honest.
6. Demonstrating innovative or creative ideas.
   a. Follows a variety of approaches in activities and techniques.
   b. Challenges conventional practices.
   c. Thinks differently by relying on a disparate set of resources.
7. Engaging with others at work and the community.
   a. Recognizes the value of others within the community on a regular basis.
   b. Supports others through training, identification of new resources, or forging connections across departments.
   c. Offers a pleasant personality and is someone people want to be around.
8. Getting along with others.
   a. Encourages the full participation of all team members.

    b. Excels in appointing people with complementary skills for maximum team effort.

    c. Makes sure that personal differences do not impact professional environment.

9. Learning about new technological developments.

    a. Seeks out new technological platforms and devices to improve organizational effectiveness and efficiency.

    b. Helps others overcome issues with new technology.

    c. Studies how competitors are leveraging technology.

10. Locating, organizing, and evaluating information.

    a. Demonstrates a tremendous knowledge of information sources.

    b. Draws on a variety of resources to achieve results.

    c. Seeks out new information sources to help spark creative ideas and new ways of thinking.

11. Managing and leading others.

    a. Projects self-confidence, authority, and enthusiasm.

    b. Is an inspirational leader.

    c. Exerts a positive influence on the organizational culture.

    d. Understands the difference between management and leadership and works hard at development of both skill sets.

12. Organizing and executing a plan of action.

    a. Effectively puts plans into action.

    b. Anticipates emerging opportunities.

    c. Schedules updates to ensure plan continues forward.

13. Thinking critically and analytically to solve problems.

    a. Promotes an environment conducive to creativity.

    b. Welcomes ideas, even those that are contradictory, from others.

    c. Recognizes the power of information.

14. Understanding global issues and their implications.

    a. Recognizes the key global trends impacting the organization.

    b. Works to help others understand the implications of global issues.

15. Conducting quantitative analysis.

    a. Demonstrates competency working with numbers and complete data analysis.

    b. Discusses data integrity and its importance within a study.

    c. Understands how data can help provide insight into key issues.

While employers are looking for these and other skills rest assured that they do not always understand what it is they are asking in a candidate. For example, along with communication, critical thinking is a top skill employers often look for in candidates. How does one define it though? With mentions of critical thinking in job postings doubling since 2009 it is important for you to have a few examples of critical thinking you can rely on when required to do so.[29] After you have provided one illustration ask the interviewer if that matched their definition of critical thinking. If not, use another example. The key is to fully understand the question and then be able to eloquently answer it in a clear, concise, and compelling manner. "In a global economy where quality labor with unique skills is scarce" you need to do everything you can to market your value so that the interviewer understands that you represent "quality labor with unique skills."[30]

Professional Skills Audit

Directions: Now that you have reviewed the 15 professional skills and corresponding examples, rank order them from most to least in your ability to demonstrate. Example: You manage and lead a team of 15 people and while you demonstrate other skills this is the one you would rank as number one on your list. You spend the least amount of time with quantitative data analysis so you rank that last. Example of a professional skill set in rank order:

1. Managing and leading others
2. Getting along with others
3. Collaborating with others or working as a team member
4. Organizing and executing a plan of action
5. Thinking critically and analytically to solve problems
6. Engaging with others at work and the community
7. Being flexible while managing multiple tasks
8. Communicating by listening, writing, or speaking
9. Connecting choices and actions to ethical decisions
10. Demonstrating innovative or creative ideas
11. Learning about new technological developments

12. Locating, organizing, and evaluating information
13. Understanding global issues and their implications
14. Completing assignments independently
15. Conducting quantitative analysis

Your professional skills in rank order

1. _____
2. _____
3. _____
4. _____
5. _____
6. _____
7. _____
8. _____
9. _____
10. _____
11. _____
12. _____
13. _____
14. _____
15. _____

- Why did you place these elements in this order?
- Can you provide one or two specific examples that demonstrate your competency with three different skills?
- Moving forward, what two or three skills would you like to practice on a more frequent basis? How will you go about developing each of those skills?

Conclusion

The first three steps of marketing your value challenged you to increase your self-awareness by identifying your purpose, defining success, and evaluating your traits and habits. Since we "have few formal moments of self-appraisal in our culture," it is imperative that you make self-reflection a priority as you go about navigating your career.[31] Increasing your self-awareness allows you to understand William Jennings Bryan when he said "Destiny is not a matter of chance; it is a matter of choice. It is not a thing to be waited for; it is a thing to be achieved."[32] Are you waiting for destiny or are you choosing to pursue it? Are you taking the initiative to create opportunities? It is important to remember that "we must not assume a door is closed but must push on it. We must not assume if it was closed yesterday that it's closed today."[33] In today's ever changing environment where new technologies are constantly introduced, once closed doors get opened quite frequently. For example, millions of people around the world are using new online resources like crowdfunding to push open doors and create new opportunities.

Crowdfunding platforms help people raise money for a specific cause. Over the last 5 years, "the crowdfunding industry has grown exponentially and has helped people raise billions in funding for everything from donations for personal art projects to equity financing for businesses."[34] In 2012, "crowdfunding platforms raised $2.7 billion (an 81% increase) and successfully funded more than 1 million campaigns. In your quest for opportunity and achievement, understand that a tool like crowdsourcing allows you the ability to explore your potential but it also requires you to "have the courage to run the gauntlet of uncertainty and risk vulnerability and failure."[35] Remember that as you complete the next section of this book and determine the qualities, characteristics, and words that create your personal brand.

"You are what you learn. If you don't like who you are, you have the option of learning until you become someone else. There's almost nothing you can't learn your way out of. Life is like jail with an unlocked, heavy door. You're free the minute you realize the door will open if you simply lean into it."

Scott Adams (creator of Dilbert)[36]

PART TWO

Brand

CHAPTER 4

Develop Your Positioning Material

By definition, positioning is a marketing term used to describe the process by which marketers create an image or identity in the minds of their target audience for a specific product, service, or organization. As a professional competing in today's challenging economy, you need to position yourself in the minds of prospective employers in a clear, concise, and compelling fashion. Remember, no one will advocate for you. If you want to achieve and sustain professional growth, you must work hard at making sure that you position your value as effectively as possible. Professionals at every level have an expectation that their degree or experience will have immediate and obvious value in the job market. Please understand that this is far from reality. Your degree, experience, and current position are important but what will have a greater impact on your ability to navigate your career is your ability to market your value. While it remains challenging to find employment, the real challenge is deciding how to position your value in the marketplace so that potential employers understand what it is you have to offer. This is true for the online world as well as the offline environment in which you live and work.

The offline environment consists of a variety of settings such as networking events, informal gatherings of friends, and at work itself. Perhaps the most important offline event, however, is the job interview itself. According to human resource professionals and hiring managers, having a candidate present clearly in an interview is taking up more time these days. Too many candidates are talking in circles, not listening or following directions, and rambling when they are asked how they can add value to the hiring company. Can you learn to communicate your value and position yourself in the mind of the prospective employer with purpose and intention? If not, your ability to launch a career will be at a severe disadvantage regardless of what school you attended, what your GPA was, or what you majored in. No one will care about any of that if you cannot position your value. Let's look at it another way. You may be able to write a 20-page research paper but can you discuss your value in bullet points and synthesize information to convey quickly with impact?[1] Amazingly, employers are now reporting that they've seen recent college grads "text or take calls in interviews, dress inappropriately, use slang or overly casual language, and exhibit other oddball behavior."[2] You need to realize that the interview is still a traditional, and very professional, environment. While texting, dressing inappropriately, or using casual language may be completely appropriate outside the interview, you need to realize that all of those actions, as well as you words, position yourself in the mind of that complete stranger sitting across from you wondering if you would be a good fit for their organization.

The informal approach to interviewing by recent graduates is so prevalent today compared to just a few short years ago that human resource executives have reported ruling out about one in five recent grads due to poor performance in the interview itself.[3] You may be qualified, but you positioned yourself so poorly in the mind of the prospective employer that they could not possibly offer you a job. You need to understand that the interview is a sales job. You are there to sell yourself and your value. Since we live in the age of hyperconnectivity, you also need to position yourself in the online environment as well.

In addition to the interview, your appearance online, especially on social networks, also impacts how people position you in their mind. The advent of social network sites has changed the environment for job seekers in general and college graduates specifically. Constantly remind yourself that your online behavior can hurt your reputations offline. The issue of online personal brand management is so important and pervasive. Google's Eric Schmidt said "parents will have to have the 'online privacy' talk with their children before 'the sex talk'" and "it might be when they're 8 years old, you'll be saying 'don't put that online! It'll come back to bite you!' and then have to explain why."[4] Two recent trends highlight the imperative that is online privacy and personal brand management: Firms are using social network sites to review potential candidates who have submitted credentials for a specific position and to also identify potential talent that can help them fill a vacancy.

With statistics varying, one thing is certain, more employers from almost any industry are now checking social media sites for information about a person who has applied for a job. Employers and human resource officials routinely "admit that they have made hiring decisions based on what they saw on those social networking sites, largely to the candidate's detriment. For example, HR representatives have eliminated job applicants from the screening process where their social media sites have revealed inappropriate photographs, alcohol or drug use, unsatisfactory communication skills, prejudice, dishonesty about their qualifications, derogatory comments about their previous employers or coworkers, disclosure of a former employer's proprietary information, and the like."[5]

While screening a candidate via an online search might seem harsh for some, the flip side is that "more than half of human resource professionals are tapping into social networking websites to look for in potential job candidates, a significant increase from 2008."[6] When reviewing someone's credential, approximately 56 percent of organizations reported scanning LinkedIn, Facebook, Twitter, and other professional networking sites for recruitment purposes in 2012, compared with 34 percent who used the same social networks to find new employees in 2008. "Employers are increasingly using social networking sites to engage passive job seekers—those who aren't really actively seeking new jobs but might change for the right opportunity," said Mark J. Schmit, PhD., SPHR, director of research at SHRM. "These sites can be valuable tools for organizations to find prospective employees with the specific skill sets and experience that they might not necessarily find through more traditional recruiting methods."[7]

One final note here on positioning yourself involves an important lesson of intention and interpretation. In a 2010 Baccalaureate address titled "We are What We Choose," Jeff Bezos, the CEO of Amazon, recalled a trip he took with his grandparents when he was young. During a road trip his grandmother started to smoke in the car. Bezos, a self-proclaimed precocious 10-year-old, laboriously calculated the damage to her health that his grandmother was doing by smoking. His conclusion was that, at

2 minutes per puff, she was taking 9 years off her life. When he proudly told her of his finding, she burst into tears. His grandfather stopped the car, pulled alongside the road and said to Bezos: "One day you'll understand that it's harder to be kind than clever."[8] In his speech Bezos went on to distinguish between gifts and choices. "Cleverness," he said, "is a gift. Kindness is a choice. Gifts are easy—they're given, after all. Choices can be hard." He then challenged the graduating students to think carefully about their future range of choices: "Will you be clever at the expense of others, or will you be kind?"[9]

This example illustrates the difference between the intention of your words and how someone may perceive them. You may innocently use certain words to describe your personal brand. For this example let's stick with clever since that was part of the Bezos story. During an interview you may describe yourself as a clever young graduate, providing one example after another as to how you are clever. What you have failed to do, however, is figure out if the organization even needs someone that is clever. Please understand that you must figure this out if you want to position yourself correctly. Perhaps they need someone who is kind? How can you know? Well the most effective way to find out the answer is to simply ask the person conducting the interview. You can ask a variety of questions such as: What trait or habit does the person who is looking to hire need to possess so as to be successful?

Put the technical skills aside and assume that everyone who has applied is qualified. Your biggest challenge is to determine what the employer needs. Do so by asking questions. Create a conversation about what the organization needs and why they are looking to hire someone. Once you understand whether you need to be clever or kind (or whatever it is the organization needs), you can then begin to discuss how your experience and skill set can help meet such a need.

To help you learn how to position yourself and your value in the minds of others, this chapter contains four specific tasks:

- identifying your one word
- determining your value proposition
- highlighting your success factors
- writing your personal statement

Completing these tasks is an absolute necessity if you want to learn how to leverage your experiences and communicate your value in a compelling manner so that you may live with purpose and navigate your career. Remember, human resources executives and hiring managers have an expectation that you know how to communicate your value. They read online search results, blogs, Twitter feeds, Facebook, LinkedIn, and other social media sites when researching about you so it is a strategic imperative that they like what they find. What someone discovers about you when they conduct an online search is "your brand, that's how you represent yourself."[10] Do so in the most professional of manners so you can effectively market your value and navigate your career.

Recognize Your One Word

Describing yourself in one word is one of the most difficult challenges to complete. If you do it correctly, however, it provides the focus you need as you start to learn how to communicate your value in a clear, concise, and compelling manner. The selection of a one-word descriptor is so important to the interview process and one's ability to communicate their value that LinkedIn has launched an annual list of overused LinkedIn profile buzzwords. Here is the list released in December 2013 with over 259 million members worldwide as part of their analysis:[11]

1. Responsible
2. Strategic
3. Creative
4. Effective
5. Patient
6. Expert
7. Organizational
8. Driven
9. Innovative
10. Analytical

While there were similarities around the globe among these top 10 buzzwords, LinkedIn identified some notable outliers such as the word "sustainable" in the Netherlands; "enthusiastic" in Great Britain, and "passionate" in Australia and New Zealand.[12]

Your One-Word Exercise

Step 1: In the space below write down at least 10 words to describe yourself.

Step 2: From these 10 or more words you identified above, select 5.

Step 3: Now from this list of 5 select the one word you feel as though best describes you at this point in time.

Step 4: Why did you choose this word? Do you believe you have successfully positioned this one word in the minds of others when they think of you?

Step 5: Ask 10 people to describe you in one word and compare their word against yours.

Did most people have a similar word that you selected? If not, why do you think that is? If they are choosing a word that closely resembles the one word you choose than please recognize that you are positioning yourself well in the minds of others. This is an important realization as you move forward and market your value and navigate your career.

The table below lists 50 examples of one-word descriptors.

ambitious	excellent	punctual
calm	excited	quiet
capable	fair	receptive
cheerful	friendly	responsible
confident	generous	sensitive
cooperative	gentle	sincere
courageous	happy	skillful
decisive	harmonious	stimulating
detailed	helpful	successful
determined	impartial	succinct
diligent	industrious	thoughtful
dynamic	kind	tough
efficient	knowledgeable	trustworthy

encouraging	mature	upbeat
energetic	pleasant	vigorous
entertaining	productive	willing
enthusiastic	proud	

Value Proposition Exercise

Now that you have completed the one-word exercise, you need to create a value proposition. A value proposition is a statement of seven words or less that help make you stand out from the competition. You can use your value proposition, or some variation of it, to answer any number of questions during an interview or networking event. Examples include: "How would you describe yourself in a minute or less?" "What is your greatest strength?" "Why should we hire you?" A clear, concise, and compelling value proposition contains the following design elements:

- It highlights your ability to focus: a value proposition is seven words or less because it forces you to focus on the quality of your words, not quantity. It is impolite to ramble on for more than a few minutes when answering an interview question. During an interview it is imperative to focus on what is most important and that is engaging in a conversation.
- It demonstrates preparation: a well-defined value proposition illustrates that you have given it some thought. The last thing you want to do is stumble on such an important question during an interview or networking event.
- It allows you to tell a story: a compelling statement should help spark a conversation where you can then discuss how one or more of your experiences support the words you have chosen for your value proposition.

Examples of Value Propositions (each seven words or less):

- Using keen insight to help customers.
- Relying on resiliency to transform businesses.

- Inspiring people to pursue vibrant career paths.
- Focused on collaboration and leadership development.
- Achieving progress through passion and team work.
- Global marketer dedicated to new ideas and insights.
- Helping others develop a passion for affordable wine.
- Driving innovative product design through enthusiasm.
- Experienced senior executive focused on results.
- Building relationships through empathy and concern.
- An energy provider who gets things done.
- Developing human capital to move organizations forward.
- Growing profits by increasing effectiveness and efficiency.
- Creating compelling brands across different industries.
- Action-orientated professional driven to succeed.

Step 1: Write down at least five value proposition statements you would use to describe yourself.

Step 2: Share your ideas with others and ask them if they believe any one of those statements best describes you. If you get a consensus you might want to use the one people agree upon. If not, you may need to draft a few more statements and rethink your word choice. This is a difficult exercise for many people since they stress over selecting the best words. The best thing to do is use your value proposition for a while and see how people react to it. Remember you can always change it.

Step 3: What value proposition did you decide to use?

Highlight Your Success Factors

Now that you have your one-word descriptor and seven-word value proposition, you can turn your attention to identifying your success factors. With recruiters and hiring managers inundated on a daily basis with hundreds or thousands of applicants submitting their materials, they often resort to skimming résumés. They simply lack any amount of adequate time to read each résumé word-for-word. One study suggested that recruiters and hiring managers glance at your résumé for 6 seconds.

Other research indicates that hiring managers and recruiters may spend between 30 seconds to up to 2 minutes reading your résumé. Whether it's 6 seconds or 2 minutes, "that's hardly any time to impress someone who could determine your employment future."[13] If you are unable to keep their attention they will most likely toss your résumé aside. Let's review that last sentence. The operative phrase is "if you are unable to keep their attention." Please understand that while you may have spent hours crafting your résumé it may still lack the compelling material a recruiter or hiring manager needs at that point in time. To help you grab someone's attention while they are reading your résumé, you may want to consider placing three to five success factors at the top of your first page.

Placing three to five success factors at the top of the first page of your résumé allows you to effectively market your value within seconds. "Research suggests that content elements that propel employers to immediately discard résumés include a focus on duties instead of accomplishments, while documented achievements were highly ranked among content elements that employers look for."[14] Since successful factors focus on accomplishments, you are practicing the trait of differentiating your value from the other candidates. By focusing on your accomplishments, you grab the reader's attention. Your success factors help them understand why they should call you for an interview. Success factors indirectly answer one or more of the following questions:

- What special things did this candidate do in their past that sets them apart from others?
- How well did you do your previous job?
- What specific results did you achieve in your current position?
- What were the problems or challenges that you or the organization faced and how did you overcome the problems?
- How did the company benefit from your performance?
- How did you leave your employers better off than before you worked for them?
- How have you helped your employers to:
  o make money
  o save money
  o save time

o   make work easier and more efficient

o   solve a specific problem

o   be more competitive

o   build relationships

o   expand the business

o   attract new customers

o   retain existing customers

Examples of Success Factors

- Managed and collaborated with writers, photographers, and editors to produce the campus section of the student-managed newspaper, ensuring well-written, carefully researched and edited news stories.
- Wrote stories that involved interviews, online research, and event coverage.
- Designed compelling layouts using Adobe InDesign and Photoshop.
- Worked as data analyst for a Fortune 100 company.
- Obtained a career center graduate assistantship.
- Gained advising skills on three different levels: a private baccalaureate institution, a master's degree granting institution, and a level one research institution.
- Launched major plank of strategic plan.
- Oversaw a budget of 2 million dollars and led a staff of 15.
- Presented at Michigan Career Personnel Association's (MCPA) Annual Conference, 2013.
- Managed a variety of situations in nonprofit and for-profit environments.
- Successfully increased sales by 17% for a product line within a 24-month period.

Directions: Write down at least three but no more than five success factors. You will eventually place these at the top of your résumé. For now, be sure to write down a few sentences that explain your evidence supporting each one of your success factors. You can then mention those during an interview or networking event.

Write Your Personal Statement

The fourth exercise in this chapter requires you to write a personal statement. A personal statement is a summary of your professional skills, personal traits, and experiences in 75 words or less. Why the word limit? In today's never-ending stream of information, employers have little time to read paragraphs about you and what you offer. They are busy. A brief personal statement of 75 words or less can help spark a conversation and that is your goal. You should be able to say your personal statement in 30 seconds or less. Remember, you need to do everything that you can to advocate for yourself while helping the prospective employer understand how you can help address the needs of the organization. Keeping your personal statement brief also allows you to engage others in the conversation. Let me give you an example of how this went very wrong for a recent candidate my friend interviewed.

During a recent interview for a position on my friend's team, the candidate, let's call him Jon, was tasked to "Tell us about yourself." Ten minutes later Jon ended his answer. After about one minute into his far too long of a reply, my friend stopped listening to Jon. Out of professional courtesy my friend and his staff continued the interview but Jon failed to engage them in a conversation. You must maintain the highest levels of self-awareness during an interview or networking event so as to engage others. Having a concise, compelling, and clear personal statement is an excellent tool to use. While you will want to craft your credentials to each position you are applying to, it is imperative to have a general personal statement that you can plug into your personal website as well as the Summary field of your LinkedIn profile. To create this personal statement you will need to review your Personal Assessment of Traits and Habits , your professional skills, your purpose, and the other exercises you completed in this publication.

Examples of personal statements:

Personal Statement Example #1:

With various experience in higher education, I am a disciplined and responsible young professional who is committed to excellence. Reliable and personable, I work well both individually and on teams. My passion lies in building relationships and collaborating with others. I am able to adapt effectively to any situation and establish positive environments with my outstanding communication and problem-solving skills. My ambitious attitude enables me to prioritize multiple tasks and take initiative. You can rely on me.

Personal Statement Example #2:

With diligence and motivation, I have dedicated myself to lifelong self-improvement both personally and professionally. My outstanding attention to quality and detail, together with my ability to prioritize, allows me to successfully complete independent and team-based projects through careful listening and effective communication. Over the course of my experiences I have demonstrated the ability of getting comfortable while being uncomfortable by adapting to challenging situations, resolving issues through analytical and critical thinking, and acting courageously.

Personal Statement Example #3:

As a determined and enthusiastic young professional, I strive to continuously inspire those around me on a daily basis. Driven by my ambitious mindset, influential attitude, and synergistic appreciation, I find passion in communicating and collaborating with a variety of individuals to better reach success and achievement of goals. Through my possession of outstanding decision-making and problem-solving skills, I am able to adapt effectively to any stressful situation and better encourage feelings of positivity.

Personal Statement Example #4:

I am a motivated professional who acts as a catalyst. Through my ability to approach tasks with enthusiasm and a positive attitude, I have a proven strength in leadership. My capacity to take calculated risks propels improvement and drives advancement toward goals. I combine resourcefulness, determination, and problem-solving strategies to create innovative plans of action, which I am able to carry out with my oral and written communication abilities.

Personal Statement Example #5:

Trustworthy and dependable, I am a self-starter with a passion for learning about the world and connecting with people. Through written and verbal communication, I am eager to form and nurture relationships in the professional world. My work in journalism, the nonprofit sector, and college admissions has displayed my effective interpersonal skills and pursuit of quality communication.

Personal Statement Example #6:

As a versatile, dependable, and responsible professional I enjoy working with nonprofit organizations and small businesses. Collaboration with others and personal growth are the hallmarks of my background. Becoming a reliable, adaptable, and ambitious individual has led to an increased skill set in communications, publishing, and marketing. Through my internships and employment positions, I have developed a strong sense of leadership In helping others solve problems, answer questions, and address issues.

Personal Statement Example #7:

As a smart, hardworking and driven individual, I work to achieve success through commitment while communicating my ideas to others and working with them to achieve our shared goals. When problems arise, I am able to think critically and analyze the situation to come to an effective situation. My work with children has provided me with an opportunity to create my own life and in turn support others in their efforts to do the same.

Personal Statement Example #8:

As a professional who displays energy in performing daily responsibilities, I am a motivated and engaged individual. I can adapt to challenging situations, work independently, and successfully complete individual and team projects. My professional background includes a variety of experiences that have allowed me to demonstrate my dedication to self-improvement and commitment to excellence. With a willingness to learn, coupled with an ability to take calculated risks, I strive for perfection while addressing challenges.

CHAPTER 5

Create Your Plan of Action

The next step in building a personal brand is defining your plan of action (POA). Having a personal brand without a POA as to how to move forward is counterproductive to navigating your career. Creating a POA allows you to move forward and market your value amidst the chaos of today's economy. Planning may seem trivial for some people but remember the words of Carnegie Mellon Computer Science Professor Randy Pausch, "You can always change your plan, but only if you have one."[1] A year after being diagnosed with pancreatic cancer, doctors gave him a terminal diagnosis: "3 to 6 months of good health left." He immediately thought about how to market his value and navigate his career knowing that his life had a very short time span. His presentation "*The Last Lecture: Really Achieving Your Childhood Dreams*" on September 18, 2007 became a popular YouTube video and eventually landed him on *The New York Times* best-selling list with *The Last Lecture* book.[2] To help build your plan of action, complete the following exercises:

- How Good Do You Want to Be?
- What Are Your Career Assumptions?
- Have You Assessed Your Thinking Lately?
- What Motivates You?
- Are You Open to Creating Options?
- Are You Creating Your Own Luck?
- What Is Your Vision of the Path to Success?

How Good Do You Want To Be?

By definition, challenges are things that you decide to do. You decide to run a marathon, finish college, or get a new job. Such challenges are usually difficult and success is far from assured. Fixed mindset people need to maintain a positive self-image, so rather than risk failing they will often avoid challenges and stick to what they do well. As a result, they seldom engage in situations where they feel a need to improve themselves. Challenges are frequently viewed negatively, instead of as an opportunity for personal growth.

Growth mindset individuals, however, view failure in a far more positive light, see it as a chance to improve, and ask themselves the question that Paul Arden challenged readers to answer: "How good do you want to be?" in *It's Not How Good Your Are, It's How Good You Want to Be*. If you do fail to understand the answer to that question, it may be difficult to embrace challenges that you need to address to succeed in life. In the end, growth mindset people work hard at answering the question and embrace life's challenges along the way.

Jon Hamm is an American actor and director who asked himself "how good do I want to be?" and then practiced a growth mindset to answer the question. Both of Hamm's parents died before he was 21 years old. After graduating from the University of Missouri in 1993 with a Bachelor of Arts degree in English, Hamm returned to his high school to teach eighth grade acting. With Paul Rudd as a friend and a desire to act for a living, Hamm moved out to Los Angeles in 1995, with an automobile and $150. His older appearance made it difficult to find employment, and after 3 years he was dropped by the William Morris agency. A fixed mindset individual would have viewed such a development as a failure. Instead, Hamm continued working as a waiter and set his 30th birthday as a deadline to succeed in Hollywood.

His belief was that "You either suck that up and find another agent, or you go home and say you gave it a shot, but that's the end of that. The last thing I wanted to be out here was one of those 45-year-old actors with a tenuous grasp of their own reality, and not really working much."[3] Eventually he landed the role of the advertising executive Don Draper in the AMC drama series Mad Men, which premiered in July 2007. The Draper role earned him a Golden Globe Award for Best Actor in a Drama Series in 2008. Reflecting back upon his experiences Hamm believes that "Losing both parents at a young age gave me a sense that you can't really control life—so you'd better live it while it's here. All you can do is push in a direction and see what comes of it."[4] Hamm asked himself 'how good do I want to be?' and then kept pushing until he answered that question. Have you?

- How good do you want to be?
  o Quite good
  o Good
  o Very good
  o The best in your field
  o The best in the world
- Why do you want to be this good?
- What skills or traits would it take to be the best in your field or even the best in the world?

What Are Your Career Assumptions?

Step 1: Current Assumptions. Choosing a career path is built upon assumptions. What are your career assumptions? Have you ever thought about your assumptions and how they impact your decision to look for or even apply to a specific job? Following is the list of assumptions that people often make regarding their job prospects:

- I've done this for so long, I can't change.
- A fabulous career that makes a difference in the world is for someone else, not me.
- The reason I'm not happier in my work is someone else.
- I'd never make this kind of money if I changed to something more meaningful.
- Other people are more creative, talented, and innovative – I don't have much to offer.
- I'm tired of the corporate world, but I don't have what it takes to go a different route.

- Which of these can you relate to? Why do you think that is?

- What are some other assumptions you might have?

- Where did those assumptions originate? (e.g., parents, teachers, colleagues, managers, friends, others, media)

- What, if anything, have you done to verify each assumption?

  Step 2: <u>True/False quiz</u>. Write down true or false next to each of the following statements related to careers, jobs, and today's global marketplace:

1. Perceptions of the variations in economic success among graduates in different majors are exaggerated.[5]
2. History majors who pursued careers in business ended up earning, on average, just as much as business majors.[6]
3. Education is important determinant of income but not the only one.[7]
4. Employers routinely agree that a candidates' demonstrated capacity to think critically, communicate clearly, and solve complex problems is more important than their undergraduate major.[8]
5. In industries across the board, employers viewed an internship as the single most important credential for recent grads – more than where you went to school and what you majored in.[9]
6. Getting to the corner office has more to do with leadership talent and a drive for success than graduating with a specific degree from a prestigious university. No one degree is necessarily better than another when moving up the corporate ladder or earning potential.[10]
7. Employers say that future workplaces need degree holders who can come up with novel solutions to problems and better sort through information to filter out the most critical pieces.[11]
8. To succeed in today's hypercompetitive market, it will be counterproductive to simply to carry on with the current stimuli policies, management strategies, and curricular approaches.[12]
9. Companies are more strict about who they hire today than in previous years because of the economy and the cost of hiring. Today, it's not just about finding the person that can do the job, but finding someone who can fit into the corporate culture.[13]

10. Hiring managers complain that they often find today's college graduates lacking in interpersonal skills, problem solving, effective written and oral communication skills, the ability to work in teams, and critical and analytical thinking.[14]

11. One basic tenet of learning is that deep, sustainable development comes from a process that includes an experience of disequilibrium followed by a period of reflective meaning-making.[15]

12. The global digital and technological revolutions during the last two decades have completely disrupted the way we live, communicate, work, and do just about everything else. Today's business environment is volatile, uncertain, and increasingly complex.[16]

13. The problem is that the global marketplace is ever-changing, and today's jobs do not necessarily mean they will be here tomorrow. Every year, more than 30 million Americans work in jobs that did not exist in the previous quarter.[17]

14. As the digital and technological revolutions continue to disrupt career paths, it is important to recognize that today's business environment is volatile, uncertain, and increasingly complex.[18]

15. The top 10 in-demand jobs in the future don't exist today. We are currently preparing students for jobs that don't yet exist, using technologies that haven't been invented, in order to solve problems we don't even know are problems yet.[19]

16. The most important factor employers look at when deciding who to hire is interview performance because they want to make sure that the student will be a good fit for their organization.[20]

17. "A manager can read you the moment you walk in the door. The most successful applicant is the one who walks into every interview with his/her hand outstretched for a handshake, has done his/her homework on the interviewer and company, and is dressed to fit effortlessly into the culture of the workplace.[21]

18. Competitiveness for jobs is at an all-time high and individuals are under unprecedented pressure to develop their own abilities more highly than ever before.[22]

19. The real challenge isn't just finding a job; it's deciding how to apply these very fundamental skills to the line of work you choose for

yourself. But take note: employers aren't going to figure it out for you. You have to figure it out for yourself.[23]

20. Even in tough times there are jobs to be had, but applicants have to work far harder to get an employer's attention. They need to market themselves better and consider a broader range of employers.[24]

Step 3: Evaluate your answers. How many statements did you select as false? Would you be surprised to learn that all of the statements are true? The endnote provides research that supports each statement.

Step 4: Compare these 20 statements with your assumptions. Knowing these statements are supported with research, does that change your assumptions about finding a job or a career path? Explain.

Step 5: Top five statements. Review the 20 statements and select the 5 that you feel as though have the most impact on your thinking. Why did you select these five?

Have You Assessed Your Thinking Lately?

The Thinking Assessment Questionnaire consists of 10 questions that challenge you to examine how you think. Assessing the process by which you think is critical to survive and thrive in any organizational culture. Each question is stated below with a brief explanation.

1. **How often do you use the 80/20 rule (devote 80 percent of energy to the most important 20 percent of daily activities?**
   a. Successful thinkers manage to devote 80 percent of their energy to the most important 20 percent of their activities. You are not superman and you can't be everywhere at the same time and have a life that is satisfying in every aspect. You need to divide and conquer as well as be focused and work without any distractions.
      i. Spend time on a regular basis to identify what the 20 percent is in your life. As you mature, this will most likely change. Realize this and make it part of your routine. Remember, professional development is directly related to personal

growth, so in order to grow one must recognize what is required.

2. **How often do you discipline your mind and thought process to think in a positive light?**

   a. Disciplining your mind to think in a positive light toward success is vital for accomplishing any goal. The human mind is automatically negative and lazy, so what you need to do is flip those thoughts around and turn them into positive and optimist pushes for your own triumph. Convince yourself that success makes sense and each day it will seem like more of a possibility.

      i. Increase your self-awareness, so that you can catch yourself thinking in a negative light before you finish processing your ideas. Also realize the types of behavior others around you exhibit. For example, when you have a positive idea about something and share it with a friend or family member, do they tend to turn it into a negative? Do they ignore your ideas? Or do they support you despite their disagreement? Being aware of how others treat our ideas is a cornerstone of personal growth and professional development.

3. **How open are you to new ideas and people that challenge you to think differently in order to achieve your goals?**

   a. Successful thinkers understand that they need to be challenged on a regular basis. If they just surround themselves with people who think like them, they rarely develop.

      i. Examine how often you are open to new ideas. We tend to get into physical and cerebral routines and lull ourselves to sleep, thinking we are in great shape when it comes to thinking, but the reality is much different.

4. **How often do you execute an idea even when you do not have all of the information required?**

   a. Henri Bergson once wrote "Think like a man of action, act like a man of thought." Everyone has ideas every single day, but those who are successful decide to actually execute those ideas because they are confident in themselves and they are able to make their dreams a reality.

      i. Keep a running list of your ideas and track how many you translate into action. What percentage of time do you translate your idea into reality?

5. **How often do you put your ideas through iterations and revisions in order to improve your initial thought?**

   a. Thoughts and ideas need to be shaped and specified until they have enough substance to be brought to life. These people don't just act sporadically when something good comes to mind. They first think it through and make sure the idea stands the test of clarity and questioning.

      i. Successful thinkers understand that their process will involve several iterations before the finished product is ready for public view. Do you have an idea and just call it quits or do you keep playing with that idea over an extended period of time to polish it?

6. **How often do you seek input from others when processing new ideas?**

   a. Thinking with others often yields higher returns. Brainstorming sessions often serve as catalysts when processing new ideas.

      i. Successful thinkers not only understand that their ideas are good but also realize that perhaps others have something valuable to add as well. Are you open to seeking input or do you just charge ahead without any regards for the opinions, thoughts, and ideas of others? Do you actively seek input from others, especially those you might not work with on a regular basis?

7. **How often do you reject popular thinking and pursue ideas that make you uncomfortable for thinking outside of the box?**

   a. People tend to base their actions off popular thinking and what society has deemed as sensible. Successful people understand that what is acceptable to the masses is mostly pedestrian and that they need to think outside the box to really satisfy themselves. They understand that they must feel comfortable with the uncomfortable and not settle with what at first seems most secure and less risky. These people think for themselves, even if no one they know agrees with them. If they believe in it, their own desire is enough for them to get started.

    i. Have you recently challenged what is generally acceptable? What has been the reaction by others when you reject popular thinking? Does such a reaction make you feel uncomfortable? Did you back down and give in to what everyone else believes is the right way to think about a specific subject?

8. How often do you plan ahead and work toward achieving a specific outcome (while leaving some room for spontaneity?)

    a. When you decide to think with strategy, there is less of a margin for error. Simply having vague ideas of where you are and what you want to accomplish will get you nowhere. The keys to being strategic: 1. Break the issue down. 2. Ask why the problem needs to be solved. 3. Identify the key issues. 4. Review your resources. 5. Put the right people in place. Henry Ford once said, "Nothing is particularly hard if you divide it into smaller parts."

        i. Do you manage organically and let things evolve on a daily basis or do you have some idea of what you want to accomplish? Managing organically is fine as long as everyone else is on board. Successful thinkers, however, usually plan out the details and understand that events do arise so they adjust accordingly.

9. How often do you engage in stimulating environments, situations, or ideas that help jump start your ability to think differently?

    a. Thinking differently requires taking different approaches to solving problems. To become more accustomed to thinking outside of the box, start engaging in activities that are more conducive to your knowledge of the world rather than your own comfort. You need to break out of your normal day-to-day routine and open your mind up to new, intellectually stimulating experiences. This will help open your mind up to new ideas about how to live a more fruitful and valuable life.

        i. Is your daily routine prohibiting you from seeing things differently? Dedicate a specific part of each week to stimulating environments, situations, or ideas that will serve as a catalyst for the ideas you are currently thinking about as well as possibly creating new ones. Routine has its place and is very useful, but if it is used too much it becomes a detriment to personal growth and professional development.

10. How often do you think long-term and process the implications of events today on tomorrow?

a. Successful thinkers understand that their actions today have implications tomorrow. As they think through an idea, their process includes an examination into the potential implications on themselves, their organization, as well as others involved.

i. When you process an, idea how often do you think about the long-term implications? How much time do you spend thinking about the long-term implications? Do you find yourself worried about the short-term implications? Does that thinking hinder your ability to think long-term?

The Thinking Assessment Questionnaire (TAQ) below asks you to assess how you think and consists of 10 questions. Rate your response using the scale: never, seldom, frequently, or always. Be sure to complete TAQ on a routine basis, so that you can track your progress on how you are thinking.

Question	Never	Seldom	Frequently	Always
1. How often do you use the 80/20 rule (devote 80% of energy to the most important 20% of your daily activities?				
2. How often do you discipline your mind and thought process to think in a positive light?				
3. How open are you to new ideas and people that challenge you to think differently in order to achieve your goals?				
4. How often do you execute an idea even when you do not have all of the information required?				
5. How often do you put your ideas through iterations and revisions to improve your initial thought?				
6. How often do you seek input from others when processing new ideas?				

Question	Never	Seldom	Frequently	Always
7. How often do you reject popular thinking and pursue ideas that make you uncomfortable for thinking outside of the box?				
8. How often do you plan ahead and work toward achieving a specific outcome (while leaving some room for spontaneity?)				
9. How often do you engage in stimulating environments, situations, or ideas that help jump start your ability to think differently?				
10. How often do you think long-term and process the implications of events today on tomorrow?				

What Motivates You?

Seventy-one percent of American workers are "not engaged" or "actively disengaged" in their work, are emotionally disconnected from their workplaces, and are less likely to be productive. [25] That leaves nearly one-third of American workers who are "engaged," or involved in and enthusiastic about their work and contributing to their organizations in a positive manner. [26]

Recent research has clearly illustrated that intrinsic motivation factors, such as intellectually stimulating work, learning new skills, having fun, and feeling valued, are all stronger predictors of job performance than extrinsic motivation elements such as salary, bonus, or some other financial reward.

"The more people focus on their salaries, the less they will focus on satisfying their intellectual curiosity, learning new skills, or having fun, and those are the very things that make people perform best." [27]

Psychologist Frederick Herzberg identified work factors (such as wages, job security, or advancement) that made people feel good about their jobs and others that made them feel bad about their jobs. He surveyed workers, analyzed the results, and concluded that to understand employee *satisfaction* (or *dissatisfaction*), he had to divide work factors into two categories:[28]

- *Motivation factors:* Factors including promotional opportunities, opportunities for personal growth, recognition, responsibility, and achievement are strong contributors to job satisfaction.
- *Hygiene factors*: Factors including quality of supervision, pay, company policies, physical working conditions, relations with others, and job security are *not* strong contributors to satisfaction, but that must be present to meet a worker's expectations and prevent job dissatisfaction.

Fixing problems related to hygiene factors may alleviate job *dissatisfaction*, but it won't necessarily improve anyone's job *satisfaction*. To increase satisfaction (and motivate someone to perform better), you must address motivation factors. Is the work itself challenging and stimulating? Do employees receive recognition for jobs well done? Will the work that an accountant has been assigned help him or her to advance in the firm? According to Herzberg, motivation requires a twofold approach: eliminating dissatisfiers and enhancing satisfiers.

Questions:

- Which set of factors do you find most attractive and why?
- While you may like factors from each side, please select either hygiene OR motivation factors and decide which set you find more attractive.
- Looking back on previous jobs, did hygiene or motivation factors cause you to leave?

What Life Approach Will You Use?

After you have answered the question "how good do you want to be?", you can then figure out what life approach you will use to achieve the level of greatness you have identified. In the global best-selling fictional novel *The Alchemist*, author Paulo Coelho states, "when people are young, they are not afraid to dream. But as time passes, a mysterious force begins to convince them that it will be impossible to realize their Personal Legend."[29] A Personal Legend is one's destiny. It is the key to living a life of purpose and intention. Through the eyes of a literate boy shepherd, Santiago, *The Alchemist* proposes that the pursuit of one's Personal Legend exists as life's primary spiritual demand. As a result, the idea that people should live in the singular pursuit of their dreams emerges as the primary theme of *The Alchemist*. Have you allowed the mysterious force to convince you that it is impossible to realize your Personal Legend? How much time have you allowed yourself to identify your Personal Legend?

Individuals are often told: "follow your passion," do "what you love," what you were "meant to do," or "make your dreams come true." Unfortunately, for recent college graduates, recent events demonstrate that their current thinking may be at odds with reality. For example, two thirds of the students in college now think they're going find a job that allows them to change the world, half within 5 years.[30] Might such a task simply be too much? As one observer noted, "In today's challenging economy doesn't such a way of thinking just set young people up to fail?"[31] The statistics are rather clear on this point. The vast majority of recent graduates and those in the near future as well will not be employed in a job that is related to their passion or one that will allow them to change the world.

You can follow your passion and help change the world, but you will most likely need to do that on your own time. If you can find a job that allows you to do all that, you indeed would be in the minority. Assessing your life approach can also help you get more out of your college experience. Unfortunately, "too many students fail to engage in the process of figuring out what they want to get out of their entire college experience."[32] Why is this? One reason is because they have insufficiently determined their life approach. Clarity on our approach to life has a direct correlation to our ability to get things done. And remember, there is no such thing as luck. Luck, or as some people would define it, success, is the intersection of preparation and opportunity. Do everything you can to prepare yourself for a future opportunity.

A life approach is defined as the way someone thinks about themselves and the world around them. A life approach illustrates to ourselves and to those around us how we address issues, answer questions, and resolve problems. A life approach allows us insight into our priorities and transforms our thoughts into actions. While there are many life approaches, here is a brief explanation of just six of them:

- *FORGING*: You believe you create your life and use effective thinking to translate your vision into reality by taking action. Used most often by people who are open to new ideas, and who take action and seek to grow both personally and professionally. Those who practice forging as a life approach believe what George Bernard Shaw once said, "Life isn't about finding yourself. Life is about creating yourself." Forging requires you to be cognizant of the chaos, aware of the opportunities, and dedicated to making progress amidst life's challenges.

- *EXPECTATION*: When you live your life to meet the expectations of others. Sometimes it is helpful to have people expect much from you. When parents, teachers, or managers expect you to do the right thing that can help you accomplish goals. When those expectations dictate your life, however, you need to ask yourself if they run counter to your own dreams and goals. An expectation life approach mandates that you act a certain way and that dictates all your actions regardless of your own goals. Often used by those who do not want to disappoint others or who lack the ability to follow a more proactive life approach such as forging. Students and young people in their 20s often use this approach most often for fear of letting their parents or family members down regarding a professional or personal issue.

- *RANDOM*: You think that whatever is going to happen will happen regardless of what you do, how much effort you use, or how much you learn. The random life approach is used by those with low self-esteem as well as those who have a carefree attitude toward life. It's good to be prepared for whatever opportunity comes along your path but a random life approach could be interpreted as one with little or no drive and that is something you need to understand as you build your personal brand. While randomness happens, it is important to understand just how often you rely on it.

- *INERTIA*: You feel sorry for yourself and sit around doing nothing for long periods of time, yet expect something to happen. People use this life approach when they want others to feel sorry for them. Those that practice this life approach might even have a job to earn money but they do little else to help themselves. They focus on the need to make money to pay the bills instead of how they can leverage their other nonwork time to do the things that they love to do.

- *BUS STOP*: You think someone else will come along and tell you what to do or where to go. Used by those who lack confidence and are content with letting others make decisions. Waiting for others to take care of our problems often results in a frustrating life approach. Many college students use this bus stop approach. They mistakenly believe that since they are at the "right" bus stop, or school, all they have to do is wait for the career bus to come along and pick them up upon graduation. It's important to realize that such an approach is ill-suited to help people achieve and sustain growth today.

- *PRIVILEGED*: You think you are privileged and deserve everything with no effort. Used by those who rely on connections and often lack a strong work ethic. People who use this life approach are subject to what Barry Switzer once observed: "Some people are born on third base and go through life thinking they hit a triple."

Questions:

- Which life approach have you used in the past?
- Which one would you like to use moving forward?
- Do you know people that practice each of the six life approaches?

Using the Jungle Gym to Create Career Options

In her book *Lean In: Women, Work and the Will to Lead*, Sheryl Sandberg borrows a career development metaphor of the jungle gym from *Fortune* magazine editor Pattie Sellers. According to Sandberg, "A jungle gym scramble is the best description of my career since I could never have connected the dots from where I started to where I am today."[33] The jungle gym metaphor offers a different approach to career development than the traditional corporate ladder for a variety of reasons:

- *Movement:* the jungle gym allows you to move up, down, and sideways, whereas the ladder only allows you to move up and down. Having the flexibility of a jungle gym is an absolute necessity in today's challenging job market.
- *Collaboration:* the jungle gym allows you to work with others, while the ladder only offers you the opportunity to walk over someone to get to the next step.
- *Foundation:* the jungle gym has a wide base and therefore allows for a stronger foundation as compared to the ladder that has two legs and is subject to wind, shifts in weight, or unpaved surfaces.
- *Achievement:* the jungle gym allows more than one person to sit at the top, while the ladder only has room for one person.

Questions:

- What is your initial reaction to the jungle gym metaphor for career development?
- Are you currently climbing the ladder or have you found yourself on the jungle gym?
- Do you prefer the ladder or the jungle gym metaphor for your career? Why?
- Which one would you rather utilize as you advance throughout your career and why?

Are You Creating Your Own Luck?

As you build your POA it will be good to remember some of the life lessons cartoonist Scott Adams learned while navigating his career. In his 2013 book *How to Fail at Almost Everything and Still Win Big: Kind of the Story of My Life*, Adams discusses how he pursued a strategy of managing his opportunities in a way that would make it easier for luck to find him. He summarized his book with this list:

- Good ideas have no value because the world already has too many of them. The market rewards execution, not ideas.
  - o Which do you find yourself doing more of: thinking about ideas or executing ideas?
- Goals are for losers. Focus on the process.
  - o Are you so focused on the goal that you forget the process?
- If you want success, figure out the price, then pay it.
  - o Are you willing to pay the price?
- The most important metric to track is your personal energy.
  - o Do you maintain a relatively fit lifestyle so you can maintain a high level of personal energy?
- Every skill you acquire doubles your odds of success.
  - o What is the last skill you have worked on during the last week or month?
- Luck can be managed, sort of.
  - o Luck is where opportunity meets preparedness. You need to be prepared for any opportunity that comes along your path. Are you prepared? Are you open to new opportunities?

The exercises in this chapter challenge you to look at yourself. Living a life of purpose and successfully navigating your career demands that you know yourself on many levels and in various dimensions. During an interview on *Inside the Actors Studio*, George Clooney referred to the importance of knowing yourself when he said that actors take "risks that a lot of people wouldn't take because it's embarrassing." Auditions, rejections, or bad roles are humiliating but are part of the process of navigating their career. Since "humiliation is one of the greatest fears in the world, and actors risk humiliation every time they go to an audition," you need to know if you have the level of confidence required to persevere.[34] Self-awareness is a prerequisite to successfully marketing your value and navigating your career.

What Is Your Vision of the Path to Success?

This last exercise as you create your plan of action requires you to envision the road to success. The adjacent illustration compares "what people think the path to success looks like" to "what it really looks like."

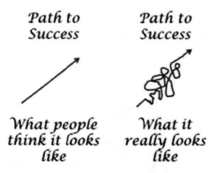

- What does your path to success look like?
- Why do people think the path to success is a straight line?
- What skills or experiences can you rely on to navigate the path to success and how it really looks like?

CHAPTER 6

Manage the Chaos

Having a stable or predictable career path in today's chaotic global marketplace continues to create high levels of uncertainty and unpredictability. The last step in creating your personal brand is learning how to manage the chaos. If you can manage the chaos then you are more likely to navigate your career into unchartered waters. This skill is critical for your brand. But remember, the path you will travel when launching your career will take years and consist of converting stumbling blocks into stepping stones. Rest assured that the panic, insecurity, and fear that you feel are normal. Managing the chaos means taking the time to reflect and learn from each moment. Remember, "one basic tenet of learning is that deep, sustainable development comes from a process that includes an experience of disequilibrium followed by period of reflective meaning-making."[1] This will be especially true when you are trying to define what success looks like.

For some people, having kids is how they define success. For others, becoming the first in their family to graduate college is most important. Still others will define success as making six figures. When you start to feel anxious about managing the chaos to market your value and navigate a career built on purpose, relax. Know that everything takes time. As long as you are moving forward one small step at a time, that's what is most important. It's a marathon, not a sprint. "There is always another day. Don't worry about screwing up, you'll figure it out as you go along. That's how every person who's really 'made it' has done it."[2] To help you manage the chaos and figure it out as you go along, here are three design elements to use as you market your value.

- *Complexity*: Refers to the complexities of today's digital revolution, technological innovation, and speed of information distribution around the globe.
- *Climate*: Refers to the economic realities of the marketplace at this point in time. Underemployment, unemployment, inflation, and wage growth are just a few of the realities that contribute to the climate for an industry in which you work or a geographical location where you live.
- *Cultivate*: Refers to the belief in positive uncertainty that you will need to rely on amidst the chaos of today's global marketplace. Doing so allows you to accept the role of chance or serendipity on vocational decisions and career development.

Managing the chaos by understanding the complexity, recognizing the climate, and cultivating positive uncertainty will allow you to navigate the paradox of the modern world where innovative technologies allow you to learn more, create more, share more, and do more, but that also present new challenges.[3] In other words, the chaos will only continue. How you respond to these challenges will directly impact your ability to market your value, navigate your career, and live a life of purpose. Understand the complexities, be aware of the climate, and cultivate positive uncertainty to move forward and live the life you have envisioned.

Complexity

The first element you need to understand is the shift from a connected to a hyperconnected world and how that has completely disrupted the way we learn, live, and work. The resulting chaos demands that we think differently about everything and that includes career development. We are in a constant state of figuring out the rules, practices, and ethics involved with balancing both our online and offline worlds. To achieve and sustain growth amidst the chaos, organizations large and small and across all industries need employees who can help them adapt. The new challenge for leaders is "to out-think the competition in ways big and small, to develop a unique point of view about the future, and help their organization get there before anyone else does."[4] As you interview for new positions throughout your career, understand that hiring managers are asking themselves one critical question: "Can he or she help my company adapt by not only doing the job today but also reinventing the job for tomorrow?"[5] A personal brand that understands the complexity of today's global marketplace will present an image that is relevant, compelling, and savvy to potential employers. A few of the dynamics driving today's challenging economy include:

1. Information production and exchange: The *2014 Horizon Report* concluded that technological developments now allow "information to be anywhere and as a result people expect to be able to work, learn, and study whenever and wherever they want to."[6] Information is indeed everywhere and due to the advancements in social medial, mobile technology, and an ever increasing amount of user-generated content, the information production and exchange rate has reached levels never before thought possible. For example, Google CEO Eric Schmidt stated that "Every two days we create as much information as we did from the dawn of civilization up until 2003, which amounts to an estimated five exabytes of data."[7]

2. Preponderance of mobile technology: There are 2.1 billion active mobile-broadband subscriptions in the world. This accounts for approximately 29.5 percent of the global population. Mobile-broadband subscriptions have grown 40 percent annually over the last 3 years and are forecast to reach 7 billion in 2018.[8] The preponderance of mobile technology has contributed to some 300 billion instant messages and 150 billion text messages sent in 2014.[9] When the production of digital messages is coupled with the advancements in technology, it is clear that "knowledge, power, and productive capability are more dispersed than ever and have created a world where value creation will be fast, fluid, and persistently disruptive."[10] As Don Tapscott and Anthony D. Williams concluded, "only the connected will survive the power shift that is underway with a tough new rule emerging: harness the new collaboration or perish."[11]

3. Global internet penetration: A third dynamic of today's technological revolution is the tremendous increase in the global internet

penetration. During the 2000 to 2013 period, world internet usage increased over 676 percent as the number of people around the world with internet access skyrocketed from 360 million in 2000 to 2.8 billion in 2013.[12] As one observer noted, "By 2020, we'll have standard mobile network connections around the world. Billions of people will have joined the Internet and they will use their mobile devices as simply lenses to the online world."[13] World population is expected to grow by over a third, or 2.3 billion people between 2009 and 2050. If that occurs, by 2050 there will be a global population of approximately 9 billion people.[14] With more people alive it is safe to assume the number of internet users will continue to grow. For example, one estimate predicts that the Internet will have nearly 5 billion users by 2020.[15]

4. The Customization of mass production: With the advent of the industrial revolution and interchangeable parts, manufacturing moved from the craft era to the mass production era. The introduction of high-speed internet access just a few short years ago, coupled with the development of more sophisticated online software has created a new era called mass customization. "Mass customization takes the best of the craft era, when customers had products built to their specifications but only the elite could afford them, with the best of the mass production era, when everybody could get the same product because it was affordable."[16] "Companies create platforms that allow customers to serve themselves in their own way, at their own pace, in their own time, according to their own tastes."[17] For example, consumers now have the ability to design their own automobile via a company's website, download ring tones for when specific people call, and customize how they receive and pay their bills with online banking options.

5. DIY Industry: Today's innovative technologies have launched a revolution in the Do It Yourself (DIY) industry. Perhaps nowhere is this more evidence than in the field of self-publishing. People no longer need editors, cover artists, or distributors to publish their book. Due to print on demand (POD) services such as Lulu, Amazon, and a host of others, you now have nothing standing in your way between your dream of publishing a book and actually doing it. The DIY

industry for self-publishing skyrocketed as more than 391,000 titles were self-published in 2012, up 59 percent over 2011.[18]

6. The emergence of disruptive technologies: Another important dynamic of life in the 21st century is known as the introduction and implementation of a wide variety of disruptive technologies. A disruptive technology is simply when a new device is introduced to people and quickly becomes the new way of doing things. For example, current mobile phone technology helps people stay connected and has even started to change the way we live. Future disruptive technologies, however, might allow "every digital thing we own can deliver us Internet-driven content all the time."

Established Way of Doing Something	Disruptive Method
Developing roles of camera film	Digital photography
Landline telephones	Mobile phones
Desktop computers	Handheld devices
Using stores to sell products	Using websites to sell products
Printed greeting cards sent via mail	E-cards sent via email
Classrooms for teaching	Online classes
Book publishers	Print on demand websites
Digital cameras	Phones with digital cameras
Email large groups of people	Create Facebook group
Standard textbooks	Interactive E-books

Assessment: Global Technology

Directions: Each of the following questions is designed to have you conduct a self-assessment on a specific characteristic of today's global technology.

- How have you contributed to the explosion of information production and exchange during the last 2 years? What implications does this information explosion have on our personal and professional lives?
- If only the connected will survive, what are you doing to create new connections and maintain those connections

using mobile technology? Are you prepared to have your contributions stand out?

- What are you doing currently to collaborate with or sell to the almost two billion people connected via the Internet? How are you preparing for a global connection of four billion people?
- How have you benefited from the new era of mass customization that is upon us? How can you leverage this new era for professional gain?
- Have you experienced having too much choice when trying to decide on something to buy or choose? Explain.
- What do you think will happen when four billion people are connected via the Internet within the next 10 years or so?

Climate

Managing the chaos of today's challenging economy also requires you to understand the climate in which you are navigating your career. This climate has a cerebral component that involves one you think about money and wealth. For example, "in one survey 19 percent of Americans believe they have incomes within the top 1 percent. Another 20 percent believe they will be within the top 1 percent one day."[19] That adds up to a whopping 39 percent of Americans who think they will be in the top 1 percent of income earners one day. This is in stark contrast to the reality of the situation. The median full-time male worker earned $50,033 in 2013, barely distinguishable from the comparable (inflation-adjusted) figure of $49,678 in 1973.[20] This severe wage stagnation is one of the unfortunate hallmarks of today's economy. When compared to the "threshold for being in the top 1 percent in household income is $380,000 or 7.5 times median household income while for net worth," it is impossible to see how 39 percent of Americans will end up on the top 1 percent of the population.[21] This disconnect demonstrates very clearly that most people fail to understand the economic climate of today's global marketplace. When the realities are acknowledged, one's personal brand is able to better navigate the chaos.

- Global Jobs War: One element of today's climate is the global jobs war. Of the 7 billion people on Earth, there are 5 billion adults aged 15 and older. "Two billion are not looking for work while 1.2 billion people are working. Thus, there is a potentially devastating global shortfall of about 1.8 billion good jobs."[22] This also means that potential societal stress and instability lies within 1.8 billion—nearly a quarter of the world's population. "It's against this backdrop that the coming jobs war will be fought. And this new world war for good jobs will trump everything else. That's because the lack of good jobs will become the root cause of almost all world problems that America and other countries will attempt to deal with through humanitarian aid, military force, and politics. The lack of good jobs will become the cause of hunger, extremism, out-of-control migration patterns, reckless environmental trends, widening trade imbalances, and on and on."[23] In the United States, the jobs war involves 15 million unemployed people and another 15 million underemployed. Neither number, however, includes people who were working part-time because they couldn't find a full-time job. It also doesn't include people who want a job but haven't looked for work in 4 weeks.[24]

- Income Stagnation & Worker Productivity: Income stagnation coupled with an increase in worker productivity is the second part of today's climate you need to understand. Workers are producing more but earning less. Incomes for 90 percent of Americans have been stuck in neutral, and it's not just because of the Great Recession. Middle-class incomes have been stagnant for at least a generation, while the wealthiest tier has surged ahead at lightning speed.[25] In 1988, the income of an average American taxpayer was $33,400, adjusted for inflation. Fast forward 20 years, and not much had changed: The average income was still just $33,000 in 2008, according to IRS data. Although U.S. Per Capita Income (income per person) from 2000 to 2012 does increase 40.8 percent when you factor in 32.5 percent inflation over the same time period the end result is nominal growth. Combining worker productivity compounds this issue. From 1973 to 2011, worker productivity grew 80 percent and median hourly compensation, after inflation, grew by just one-eighth that amount. And since 2000, productivity has risen 23 percent while real hourly pay has essentially stagnated.[26] Meanwhile, it's been a lost economic decade for many households. According to the Center for Budget and Policy Priorities, median income for working-age households (headed by someone under age 65) slid 12.4 percent from 2000 to 2011, to $55,640. During that time the American economy grew more than 18 percent.[27]

- Pension Benefits: The percentage of the largest U.S. employers that offer a defined benefit pension plan to new salaried employees continues to fall and is another contributing factor of today's climate to comprehend. In 1998, approximately 90 percent of Fortune 100 companies offered a defined benefit plan to new salaried employees. During the following 14 years, that plummeted to 30 percent.[28] "The shift is motivated by several factors such as employers' desire to reduce retirement costs."[29]

- Free Agents: A fourth component to today's climate is the rise of free agents. Free agents are defined as individuals who work for themselves and get hired on a per diem or project basis for an organization. Prior to the emergence of the corporation as an entity that needed workers, individuals were entrepreneurs or free agents to support themselves and their families. This last hundreds of years until the corporation emerged in the 19th century. As the adjacent graph illustrates, the number of free agents dropped dramatically during the 19th and 20th centuries, but is now reversing itself as more individuals are using the free agent approach to earning money. There are numerous reasons for individuals to work as free agents,[30] but the top three are: a)To have more freedom and flexibility in my schedule; b)To follow or pursue my passion; and c) Freelancing wasn't something I planned; I fell into it. Some of the most common types of work performed by freelancers include designer, writer, web developer, business consultant, and project manager.[31] It is also important to understand that 20 percent of individuals use a multiple revenue stream approach to life as they couple free agent work with either a part-time or a full-time employment position. Sixty-five percent work as full-time freelancers, 15 percent work as part-time freelancers, 14 percent work as part-time freelancers with a regular day job, and 6 percent work as full-time freelancers with a part-time day job.

- Virtual Work: The growing number of employees working from home is another aspect of today's climate to understand. Some 13 million people, or 9.4 percent of the working population in 2010, worked at least one day at home per week, compared with just 9.2 million people in 1997, when 7 percent worked at least partly from home. People working either entirely or partly from home were more likely to be in management and business. Those in computer, engineering, and science jobs saw among the biggest shifts homeward: "Home-based" work in these fields jumped around 70 percent from 252,000 workers in 2000 to 432,000 workers in 2010. According to Census figures, 5.8 million people or 4.3 percent of the U.S. workforce worked from home *most* of the week in 2010—an increase of about 1.6 million since 2000.[32] The top reasons employees want to work from home (including both federal employees and the private sector) are:
  - Avoid commute (63%–71%)
  - Greater flexibility (49%–66%)
  - Save money (28%–31%)[33]

Even half-time home-based work accounts for savings of more than $10,000 per employee per year as a result of increased productivity, reduced facility costs, lowered absenteeism, and reduced turnover. Employees save somewhere between $1,600 to $6,800 and 15 days of time once used driving to work or taking public transportation. It's no surprise then that 47 percent of people who have the option to telework are "very satisfied" with their jobs, compared to 27 percent of those who are office-bound.[34]

- Multiple Revenue Streams: Relying on multiple revenue streams is another critical element of today's climate. In September 2014 nearly 2 million Americans were working multiple part-time jobs; an increase of 300,000 more people than 10 years ago.[35] "In a tough economy when many people are dealing with cutbacks in hours or pay, it's not unusual to find people who need to work more than one job." It's also important to note that some people work a second job since it allows them a chance to pursue their passion or purpose on a much larger scale than their day job. Examples include the musician who performs on a local circuit or a yoga teacher who teaches at night or the weekends; both rely on a day job to pay most of the bills but pursue a life of purpose when and where possible.

- Happiness: The last aspect of today's climate mentioned here is workplace happiness. Only 48 percent of Americans are happy at work. That's a significant decline from 61 percent when first measured in 1987, almost 30 years ago.[36] The drop in workers' happiness can be partly blamed on the worst recession since the 1930s, which made it difficult for some people to find challenging and suitable jobs. But worker dissatisfaction has been on the rise for more than two decades, hence contributing to workplace unhappiness. As you navigate your career amidst the chaos it is important to understand this. Also realize that happiness is a choice. All too often people allow circumstances or others to influence their level of happiness. While it's true that levels of employee satisfaction and unhappiness are on the rise, it is equally true that you have a choice in your happiness. What will you decide?

Economic Climate Assessment

Assessing your knowledge of the economic climate is essential as you navigate your career. Doing so can help you manage your expectations regarding both money and employment. For example, "the American middle class, long the most affluent in the world, has lost that distinction. While the wealthiest Americans are outpacing many of their global peers, citizens of other countries have received considerably larger raises over the last three decades."[37] To make matters worse, incomes have remained stagnant for American workers for decades. "After adjusting for inflation, U.S. median household income is still 8 percent lower than it was before the 2008 global recession and essentially unchanged since 1988."[38]

The economic picture is equally bleak for recent college graduates as only 15 percent of those who graduated in 2013 said they expected to earn less than $25,000 a year, while 32 percent of the 2011 and 2012 graduates earn $25,000 or less.[39] Millions of more experienced workers, however, know the plight of low pay as well. Of the 130 million jobs in the United States, 18 million pay less than $10 an hour and a startling 63 million pay between $10 and $20. Add it all up and you've got 81 million jobs (out of 130 million), or 62% of the population, earning less than $20 as an hourly wage.[40]

Here is the breakdown of U.S. jobs by hourly wage:

Number of U.S. Jobs (in millions)	Percentage of all U.S. Jobs	Hourly Salary	Est. Annual Salary
18	14%	Less than $10/hour	$20,800 or less
63	48%	Between $10 to $20/hour	Between $20,800 and $41,600
27	21%	Between $20 to $30/hour	Between $41,600 and $62,400
13	10%	Between $30 to $40/hour	Between $62,400 and $83,200
10	7%	Over $40/hour	$83,200 or more
131 million jobs	100%		

The following assessment will test your knowledge about the U.S. economy as it relates to wages and other relevant data you need to know as you manage your expectations and navigate your career.

Assessment: The Income & Employment Quiz (Answers found on next page)

1. What percentage of U.S. households has a total combined income of $50,000 or less?

   31 percent, 41 percent, 51 percent, 61 percent, 71 percent

2. What percentage of U.S. households has a total combined income of $100,000 or more?

   5 percent, 9 percent, 12 percent, 17 percent, 23 percent

3. What percentage of U.S. individuals earn $50,000 or less?

   41 percent, 49 percent, 55 percent, 66 percent, 71 percent

4. What percentage of U.S. individuals earn $100,000 or more?

   7 percent, 12 percent, 15 percent, 22 percent, 29 percent

5. The average balance in all 50 million 401(k) retirement accounts is just over $120,000.

   True

   False

6. People within 10 years of retirement have saved an average of only $78,000, and more than a third of them have less than $25,000.

   True

   False

7. Approximately one-third of U.S. workers have no retirement plan at all.

   True

   False

8. Today's students will have approximately 5 to 7 jobs by the time they are 38 years of age.

   True

   False

9. About 284,000 Americans with college degrees were working minimum wage jobs last year, according to the Wall Street Journal. That's 70 percent more college grads working for the minimum wage than 10 years ago. Still, the number is down from its 2010 high of 327,000.

   True

   False

10. The number of people with a Masters who received food stamps almost tripled from 101, 682 to 293,029, and the number of PhD.s on public assistance substantially increased from 9,776 to 33,655 during the last few years.

    True

    False

Answers to The Income & Employment Quiz:

- Question #1: 51 percent of U.S. households have a total combined income of $50,000 or less?[41]
- Question #2: 17 percent of U.S. households have a total combined income of $100,000 or more?[42]
- Question #3: 71 percent of U.S. individuals earn $50,000 or less?[43]
- Question #4: 7 percent of U.S. individuals earn $100,000 or more?[44]
- Question #5: False. The average balance in all 50 million 401(k) retirement accounts is just over $60,000.[45]
- Question #6: True. People within 10 years of retirement have saved an average of only $78,000, and more than a third of them have less than $25,000.[46]
- Question #7: True. 31% of U.S. workers have no retirement plan at all.[47]
- Question #8: False. Today's students will have approximately 10 to 12 jobs by the time they are 38 years of age.[48]
- Question #9: True. About 284,000 Americans with college degrees were working minimum wage jobs last year, according to the Wall Street Journal. That's 70 percent more college grads working for the minimum wage than 10 years ago. Still, the number is down from its 2010 high of 327,000.[49]

- <u>Question #10: True.</u> The number of people with a Masters who received food stamps almost tripled from 101, 682 to 293,029, and the number of PhD.s on public assistance substantially increased from 9,776 to 33,655 during the last few years.[50]

Cultivate

The third and final element that you need to understand as you manage the chaos is the paradigm of cultivating positive uncertainty. There is no doubt that life is uncertain. When navigating their career most people want to obtain some level of certainty that their position, department, and organization will be around for an extended period of time. This is difficult in today's economy. When navigating your career today you need to look beyond those positions that are probable and challenge yourself to consider those that are possible. Developing a career path based on the probable will severely limit your options. Charting a career based on what is possible allows you to travel down paths previously unimagined. Acknowledge that the future involves ambiguity and paradox. Once you accept that the future is full of ambiguity and paradox you can then realize that "one does not know some things, cannot always see what is coming, and frequently will not be able to control it. Being positive and uncertain allows one to be able to act when one is not certain about what one is doing."[51] Practicing positive uncertainty allows you to navigate amidst the chaos, adjust to the disruption, and live a life of intention and purpose. As an illustration of just how uncertain the future is, one study estimated that 47 percent of the U.S. job market is at risk of being automated by 2034.[52] In less than 20 years, close to half of the jobs in America could be subjected to algorithms, robotics, or yet to be invented technologies. Entire industries are subject to change in the future. All the more reason to practice positive uncertainty as it will help you navigate such disruption.

Ten Steps to Practice Positive Uncertainty

1. <u>Energy</u>: Devote 80 percent of energy to the most important 20 percent of daily activities. Successful thinkers manage to devote 80 percent of their energy to the most important 20 percent of their

activities. You are not superman and you can't be everywhere at the same time and have a life that is satisfying in every aspect. You need to divide and conquer as well as be focused and work without any distractions. Spend time on a regular basis to identify what the 20 percent is in your life. As you mature this will most likely change. Realize this and make it part of your routine. Remember, professional development is directly related to personal growth, so to grow one must recognize what is required.

2. Discipline: Discipline your mind and thought process to think in a positive light. Disciplining your mind to think in a positive light toward success is vital for accomplishing any goal. The human mind is automatically negative and lazy, so what you need to do is flip those thoughts around and turn them into positive and optimist pushes for your own triumph. Convince yourself that success makes sense and each day it will seem like more of a possibility. Increase your self-awareness so that you can catch yourself thinking in a negative light before you finish processing your ideas. Also realize the types of behavior others around you exhibit. For example, when you have a positive idea about something and share it with a friend or family member, do they tend to turn it into a negative one? Do they ignore your ideas? Or do they support you despite their disagreement? Being aware of how others treat our ideas is a cornerstone of personal growth and professional development.

3. Be Open: Remain open to new ideas and people that challenge you to think differently so as to achieve your goals. Successful thinkers understand that they need to be challenged on a regular basis. If they just surround themselves with people who think like them, they rarely develop. Examine how often you are open to new ideas. We tend to get into physical and cerebral routines and lull ourselves to sleep thinking we are in great shape when it comes to thinking, but the reality is much different.

4. Take Action: Execute an idea even when you do not have all of the information required. Henri Bergson once wrote "Think like a man of action, act like a man of thought." Everyone has ideas every single day but those who are successful decide to actually execute those ideas because they are confident in themselves and their ability to

make their dreams a reality. Keep a running list of your ideas and track how many you translate into action. What percentage of time do you translate your idea into reality?

5. Revise: Place your ideas through iterations and revisions so as to improve your initial thought. Thoughts and ideas need to be shaped and specified until they have enough substance to be brought to life. These people don't just act sporadically when something good comes to mind. They first think it through and make sure the idea stands the test of clarity and questioning. Successful thinkers understand that their process will involve several iterations before the finished product is ready for public view. Do you have an idea and just call it quits or do you keep playing with that idea over an extended period of time to polish it?

6. Seek Input: Ask others for their input when processing new ideas. Thinking with others often yields higher returns. It's like giving yourself a shortcut. That's why brainstorming sessions are so effective. Successful thinkers understand that their ideas are good but also realize that perhaps others have something valuable to add as well. Are you open to seeking input or do you just charge ahead without any regards for the opinions, thoughts, and ideas of others?

7. Get Uncomfortable: Reject popular thinking and pursue ideas that make you uncomfortable for thinking outside of the box. People tend to base their actions off popular thinking and what society has deemed as sensible. Successful people understand that what is acceptable to the masses is mostly pedestrian and that they need to think outside the box to really satisfy themselves. They understand that they must feel comfortable with the uncomfortable and not settle with what at first seems most secure and less risky. These people think for themselves, even if no one they know agrees with them. If they believe in it, their own desire is enough for them to get started. What has been the reaction by others when you reject popular thinking? Does such a reaction make you feel uncomfortable? Did you back down and give in to what everyone else believes is the right way to think about a specific subject?

8. Balance Planning with Spontaneity: Plan ahead and work toward achieving a specific outcome while leaving some room for

spontaneity. When you decide to think with strategy, there is less of a margin for error. Simply having vague ideas of where you are and what you want to accomplish will get you nowhere. The keys to being strategic: (1) Break the issue down, (2) Ask why the problem needs to be solved, (3) Identify the key issues, (4) Review your resources, (5) Put the right people in place. Henry Ford once said, "Nothing is particularly hard if you divide it into smaller parts." Do you manage organically and let things evolve on a daily basis or do you have some idea of what you want to accomplish? Managing organically is fine as long as everyone else is on board. Successful thinkers, however, usually plan out the details and understand that events do arise, so they adjust accordingly.

9. Engage: Engage in stimulating environments, situations, or ideas that help jump start your ability to think differently. Thinking differently requires taking different approaches to solving problems. To become more accustomed to thinking outside of the box, start engaging in activities that are more conducive to your knowledge of the world rather than your own comfort. You need to break out of your normal day-to-day routine and open your mind up to new, intellectually stimulating experiences. This will help open your mind up to new ideas about how to live a more fruitful and valuable life. Is your daily routine prohibiting you from seeing things differently? Dedicate a specific part of each week to stimulating environments, situations, or ideas that will serve as a catalyst for the ideas you are currently thinking about as well as possibly creating new ones. Routine has its place and is very useful but if it is used too much it becomes a detriment to personal growth and professional development.

10. Think Long-term: Process the implications of events today on tomorrow. Successful thinkers understand that their actions today have implications tomorrow. As they think through an idea, their process includes an examination into the potential implications on themselves, their organization, as well as others involved. When you process an idea how often do you think about the long-term implications? How much time do you spend thinking about the long term?

The Paradox Exercise

To cultivate positive uncertainty, H.B. Gelatt identified four major paradoxes:[53]

- Be focused and flexible about what you want.
- Be aware and wary about what you know.
- Be objective and optimistic about what you believe.
- Be practical and magical about what you do.

Questions

- Which of these four have you practiced?
- Can you write out a specific example for each one that you have practiced?
- Which one do you feel as though could benefit your career at this moment in time?
- Which one presents the biggest challenge for you to implement?
- Do you know anyone who has recently practiced one or more of the paradoxes?

Conclusion

Your personal brand needs to understand the complexity of today's global marketplace, acknowledge the realities of the economic climate, and cultivate positive uncertainty to successfully navigate your career. Building a personal brand requires one to develop their positioning material, create a plan of action, and manage the chaos. The future is uncertain. Of that there is no doubt. As you navigate your career understand that it is useful and healthy to maintain a level of uncertainty when making a career decision. Trying to create absolute order and stability is actually quite hazardous when one needs to adapt to change. The research demonstrates very clearly, however, that order and stability are seldom found in one's career trajectory.

According to the 2013 *American Express Life Twist Study*, successful professionals have four distinct career paths to success:[54]

- Life Twisters: 52 percent have a distinct life path in mind but are open to occasionally veering off that path to embrace the changes life throws their way.
- Passivists: 25 percent say they lack a life plan, go with the flow when facing life's challenges, and take a more passive approach to its twists and turns.
- Traditionalists: 13 percent of people say they have a plan laid out and have no intention of veering from it.
- Reinventionists: 11 percent are much more proactive than Life Twisters in precipitating change and intentionally work toward the goal of reinventing themselves one or more times throughout their career.

The chaos of today's job market need not be feared but rather embraced with humility and openness to its inherent possibilities. You have a blank slate that helps you understand that the journey from being to becoming has unlimited possibilities. The next series of steps will help you understand how to communicate your value to successfully transition from your current self to your possible self. Since "each person must use whatever tools are available to carve out a meaningful and enjoyable life," take advantage of the tools explained in each of the following steps so you can navigate your career and live with purpose.[55]

All my life I had been looking for something, and everywhere I turned someone tried to tell me what it was. I accepted their answers too, though they were often in contradiction and even self-contradictory. I was naïve. I was looking for myself and asking everyone except myself questions which I, and only I, could answer. It took me a long time and much painful boomeranging of my expectations to achieve a realization everyone else appears to have been born with: that I am nobody but myself.

Ralph Ellison, *Invisible Man*[56]

PART THREE

Communicate

CHAPTER 7

Design Impressive Marketing Materials

Learning how to communicate your value is the most important skill you need to develop. This is true for everyone regardless of industry, type of work, or background. You need a long-term commitment to define yourself and your purpose so as to broadcast your strengths. "Give people a reason to pay attention to you. It's your choice to do something worth talking about or not. The only people who stand out are those who want to."[1] Unfortunately, most professionals seldom practice this and, as a result, fail to realize their potential. Employers want candidates who can present a clear, concise, and compelling argument as to what they bring to an organization in terms of value, skills, and experiences. With high levels of global unemployment and underemployment in the foreseeable future, learning how to communicate your value will remain a top priority for those who want to successfully navigate their career.

Now that you have completed a variety of assessments, exercises, and a series of tasks, the final step in communicating your personal brand is creating the following list of items that will help you position yourself in the minds of others as you go about launching your career. Remember that all of these items should be updated on a regular basis as you gain new experiences. The one thing you do not want to get into the habit of doing is landing a job, and then stop marketing yourself. You should allocate time each week to market yourself no matter how much you love your job. Remember, no one will advocate for you. Use each of these items to leverage your skills, habits, and experiences so that you can live a life of purpose and work with intention. Each item is explained below and they should be done in the order in which they appear. Throughout the completion of each task it might behoove you to reflect back upon the other assessments and exercises you completed in this workbook. Remember, you have assessed your abilities, traits, and habits and have also created a personal brand, now it is time to present a clear, concise, and compelling series of communication pieces. Doing will help position yourself in the minds of others. As a college student or recent graduate it is also important for you to realize that stories can play an integral role in your ability to communicate your value. "A topsy-turvy world like the one in which we live offers us tremendous opportunities. But to tap them, you must remove the barriers and mix all of your experiences, knowledge, and skills into the precise blend that makes a new you."

Complete the following exercises to design the required marketing materials you will need to market your value and navigate your career:

- Résumé
- Cover letter
- Logo
- Personal business card
- Stories
- Personal brand website

Résumé Outline

There are as many thoughts on writing résumés as there are people who write them. My résumé format leverages your one word, value proposition, and success factors. Along with the format, this particular style is often very new for people. You may choose to use this or not. Like everything else in this workbook, this is an option. Just make sure that whatever résumé format you are using, it is communicating your value in a clear, concise, and compelling fashion.

Directions
- Use your personal statement, value proposition, and one-word description to write your résumé.
- Remember the following when revising your résumé:
  o Spell everything correctly
  o Keep it to one page
  o Include your summary of success factors at the top

o Use your work experiences to support success factors
o Use bullet points
o Include your one-word description
o Year of graduation/grades/classes are all optional
o Athletes be sure to highlight accomplishments
o Clean up your email address
o Include your cell phone number
  • *When uploading your résumé to your website, delete your cell phone number and other contact information.*
o Save your résumé using your name and date as the file (e.g., Edmondson Résumé May 2014)
o Update your résumé every time you have something to add to it. You should also update your LinkedIn and personal websites on a regular basis
o You will most likely not get a job by simply submitting a résumé. You will need to get through one or more interviews. Therefore, your mindset should be "I want this résumé/cover letter to get me an interview" and not "I want this résumé/cover letter to get me a job."

RÉSUMÉ TEMPLATE

Full Name

www.yourwebsiteaddresshere.com

Email address • address • city, state zip • telephone number

SUMMARY OF SUCCESS FACTORS

General introductory sentence (your value proposition can serve as a good idea here)

• Success factor #1
• Success factor #2
• Success factor #3

PROFESSIONAL EXPERIENCE

Internship or job or activity #1 (links to success factor #1
- Bullet point that supports success factors
- Bullet point that supports success factors

Internship or job or activity #2 (links to success factor #2
- Bullet point that supports success factors
- Bullet point that supports success factors
- Internship or job or activity #3 (links to success factor #3
- Bullet point that supports success factors
- Bullet point that supports success factors

ATHLETIC EXPERIENCE/VOLUNTEER/OTHER EXPERIENCE

- Athletic experience or activity
- Bullet point that supports success factors
- Bullet point that supports success factors

COMPUTER SKILLS AND LANGUAGE (IF APPLICABLE)

- Specific skill
- Specific skill

EDUCATION

- College and degree (up to you if you want to put GPA)

154 Words to Use in Your Résumé

Absorbed	Enhanced	Mediated	Secured
Accelerated	Enriched	Mentored	Segmented
Accomplished	Evaluated	Modernized	Selected
Achievement	Examined	Motivated	Simplified
Advanced	Exceeded	Multiplied	Skilled
Analyzed	Excelled	Negotiated	Spearheaded
Announced	Facilitate	Observed	Specified
Appraised	Financed	Obtained	Standardized
Assessed	Forecast	Operated	Streamlined
Assigned	Formulate	Organized	Strengthened
Assisted	Formulated	Originated	Structured
Attained	Fulfilled	Overhauled	Suggested
Attracted	Gained	Participated	Superseded
Balanced	Gathered	Performed	Supervised
Bargained	Generated	Pioneered	Supported
Benefited	Granted	Planned	Sustained
Bolstered	Guided	Prepared	Targeted
Boosted	Headed	Presented	Taught
Budgeted	Helped	Programmed	Tested
Closed	Hosted	Projected	Trained
Collaborated	Identified	Promoted	Transcended
Committed	Implemented	Provided	Translated
Complied	Improved	Published	Triumphed
Conducted	Improvised	Pursued	Uncovered
Consulted	Increased	Qualified	Unified
Contributed	Influenced	Quantified	United
Coordinated	Initiated	Ranked	Updated
Critiqued	Innovated	Received	Upgraded
Defined	Instituted	Recommended	Utilized
Delegated	Integrated	Redesigned	Validated
Delivered	Investigated	Reengineered	Valued
Demonstrated	Justified	Reorganized	Viewed
Designed	Launched	Represented	Witnessed
Detected	Listed	Restructured	Wrote
Developed	Lobbied	Retained	

Devoted	Maintained	Revised	
Distinguished	Managed	Safeguarded	
Diversified	Marketed	Saved	
Earned	Maximized	Scheduled	
Encouraged	Measured	Screened	

Cover Letter Outline

For many professionals the cover letter is the first contact with a potential employer. Therefore, it may behoove you to customize each cover letter as best as possible for each specific position in which you are applying. Sending out dozens of generic cover letters may be easy to do but ask yourself if that is the best way to market your value, skills, and experiences? The outline below walks you through the steps of writing a concise, clear, and compelling cover letter.

Directions

- Follow a three-paragraph format:
  - o Paragraph 1: Discuss the company, their needs, and if possible something about the position advertised. Help the reader understand that you know something about them. Don't just start talking about yourself.
  - o Paragraph 2: Now mention your skills via your personal statement and value proposition and how they can help address the issue or position you mentioned in the first paragraph.
  - o Paragraph 3: Thank them for reading the letter and have an action step for them to do. For example, "Please call me on my cell phone at _____ or email me at _____ to discuss next steps."
- Remember the following when writing your cover letter:
  - o Use 'I' sparingly—maximum between 3 and 4 times
  - o Spell everything correctly
  - o Make sure your contact information is listed
  - o Date the letter
  - o Be sure to spell the name of the company correctly

o   If you have the name of a person, be sure to spell it correctly

o   Write in complete sentences

o   Include your one word, value proposition, and success factors

o   Highlight your one word to differentiate yourself

o   Refer the reader to your website

o   *Ask for a phone interview or in-person visit for a next step. This is the goal of your résumé/cover letter submission.*

o   Thank them for their time.

Cover Letter – Example #1 (Original)

On this page, student version (version #1) represents an actual cover letter draft from a student writing to an organization looking for an internship. The student is participating in an off-campus program known as The Philadelphia Center, a global leader in experiential education. All proper names have been changed. Compare this first version with the one on the following page that has been edited. Notice the difference in structure, paragraph format, and use of the letter I.

To Whom It May Concern,

My name is Student A and I am a junior from ABC College. I am spending this semester off-campus and participating in The Philadelphia Center, and I am interested in an internship with you at XYZ Company. Next year, I plan to graduate with a degree in business and organization, with a concentration In environmental studies. I believe that XYZ Company would be a great place to intern and to get started into looking at career options. I am impressed and intrigued with the way XYZ Company got started and how you have come to be so successful over the years.

Over the past few years, I have come to realize that my interests are strongly tied to the environment. After working at a state park for two summers, I decided to take my business major and find a way to make it better fit me. At this point, I believe I am one of the few people at ABC College combining business and environmental studies. I think that my background in these areas is a great fit for XYZ Company. I also have a lot of experience working with teams and groups through the small classes at ABC College as well as being a part of the soccer team. This means

I would be more than comfortable with the small size and hardworking ethics at XYZ Company. Not only am I excited at the prospect of working at XYZ Company, I am thrilled to find a business whose ideals and morals are so similar to mine.

I appreciate you taking the time to consider me and hopefully I will get the chance to talk to you soon. I have attached my résumé and if you have any other questions please let me know. I am available Tuesday before 4 p.m. and Wednesday and Thursday all day if you are interested in scheduling an interview. Again, thank you for your time and I hope to hear from you soon.

Sincerely,

College Student

This version had 329 words and used the letter I just 18 times. It placed the focus on the individual writing the letter and ignored the mission of organization.

Cover Letter – Example #2 (Revised)

Revised version (version #2) follows the format described above in the Cover Letter Outline page.

I am a junior at ABC College majoring in business with a minor in environmental studies participating in an off-campus program—The Philadelphia Center (TPC) —this semester. While searching the placement files at TPC, I came across XYZ Company and listed it as one of my top three choices where I would like to intern 4 days a week. As the nationally recognized leader in urban farming, XYZ Company stood out as an exciting opportunity for me to learn so much more about the intersection of business and the environment. After reviewing your website one quote really resonated with me: *"A small but dedicated staff runs a multifaceted operation, including a nursery, a farm market, and a Community Supported Agriculture (CSA) program, proving that abandoned land is only abandoned if we choose to leave it that way." This philosophy, coupled with its environmental concerns, seems like an ideal placement for me and I would like to schedule an interview with you as soon as possible.*

Over the past few years, I have come to realize that my interests are strongly tied to the environment. While many factors contributed to my love of the environment, one critical experience was my work as a Campground Office Clerk at a State Park in Michigan for two summers. This experience allowed me to have an initial understanding of how to blend my interest with business and the environment. Due to my work at the State Park, as well as my experience on my college women's soccer team, I am well-suited to work collaboratively or independently. Not only am I excited at the prospect of working at XYZ Company, I am thrilled to find a business whose ideals and morals are so similar to mine. My résumé is attached for your review. Would you have time for an in-person interview Tuesday before 4:00 p.m. EST or anytime this Wednesday or Thursday?

Thank you for your time and I look forward to hearing from you.

Sincerely,

College Student

This version had 331 words and reduced the use of the letter I by 50 percent, as it appears just nine times. This version also places the focus on the organization and allows the reader to understand that the person writing the letter conducted research to understand why they would be a good fit.

Your Logo

What are the characteristics of a strong logo that conveys an impactful image? Explain and provide examples of logos that you admire. In the space below, draw your logo. Now that you have identified the one word that best describes you, what does that look like in terms of a logo? If you want to use a computer program at this point that is fine. Just be sure to keep the image file handy as you will need it when you create your personal business card or website. Be sure that your logo is directly related to your one-word description and value proposition. Remember to keep it simple as the more creative and complicated you make the logo the less likely others will understand it.

How or where can I design my own logo?

- You can visit www.printsmadeeasy.com to use their templates for your logo.
- You can also use sites like www.logomaker.com where you can design your own logo. Sites where you can customize a logo

usually have limitations as to the quality of the free logo but for a nominal fee you can purchase a higher quality logo. It's worth some time using such a site for ideas.

- You can obviously use any other site or program that you find helpful.
- You can even use PowerPoint if you understand its more creative functions.

Many people like to figure out a creative way to make their initials their logo. Others like to use the templates available. Either way is fine. Just think about what type of image you want to use and why do you want to use it? How does your logo or image link to your one-word description?

Creating a Business Card

Recent college graduates and more experience professionals alike should have a customized business card that presents their personal brand in a compelling manner as a way for people to remember you. If you have a business card that just states your name and contact information it will not differentiate yours from others. This is a tactic several colleges and universities use but it fails to convey a student's true value. Having a customized business card that highlights your value is part of a compelling story that will allow you to stand out from others, so this exercise is critically important. Having a personal business card also allows you to promote the image you want for yourself. Instead of relying on others to remember you or interpret you, you can live with intention and present the image you want. Remember, no one will advocate for you, so take it upon yourself to draft, create, and revise your personal brand as you gain more experience.

There are several online providers you could consider using to create your business card such as www.printsmadeeasy.com or www.vistaprint.com. These and other sites are usually free to use and offer templates as well as the ability to create your own business card from scratch. You could also use the templates provided in Word if you have that program or any other word processing program. The first step in this section is for you to create a business card. Refer to your personal statement, your value proposition, and your one word. It is best to develop a few different versions of your business card before selecting the one layout/design that best meets your needs at this time. As you gain more experience you will want to update your card to reflect your new skills and experience. It is very common for people change their one word and value proposition over time.

The front of your business card should have the following items:

- Select a color scheme or use one of the templates provided by the program/website you are using.
- Make sure your logo is clear for everyone to understand.
- Highlight your one word and/or value proposition.
- Include your contact information as well as your web page.

The back of your business card should have the following:

- Your value proposition
- Your website URL
- Your three success factors—but in an abbreviated form
- If possible, perhaps you can fit or create a smaller version of your logo on the back as well

NOTE: Some people have suggested that they place their picture on their business card. While that is certainly an option, how would you feel if someone made an unfavorable judgment based on your picture? Would you rather be evaluated on your personal traits and professional skills? By focusing on your success factors, value proposition, logo, and one-word description, you can better position yourself in a clear, concise, and compelling manner.

Stories

Stories are powerful tools for individuals, businesses, and organizations. "Stories are the creative conversion of life itself into a more powerful, clearer, more meaningful experience." Unfortunately "storytelling is by far the most underrated skill in business."[2] Realize that stories unite people and they help us understand each other. They provide insight into

experiences and allow us to reflect upon specific situations. We have lis-
tened to countless stories since our childhood and will continue to tell
them, and listen to them throughout our lives. Often known as "the cur-
rency of human contact,"[3] stories serve as a way to connect with strangers,
strengthen bonds with friends, and share experiences with loved ones. Due
to the technological advancements over the last 20 years, stories are found
in e-books, blogs, Tweets, movies, television shows, songs, and a host of
other mediums. Social network sites allow us to share stories easily and frequently. In short, we are comfortable with listening to, creating, and sharing stories since they have been around since the dawn of recorded history.

Realize that stories can play an integral role in your ability to communicate your value. "A topsy-turvy world like the one in which we live
offers us tremendous opportunities. But to tap them, you must remove
the barriers and mix all of your experiences, knowledge, and skills into the
precise blend that makes a new you."[4] For this task you should consider
creating two stories: a short story of 200 to 300 words and a long story
of 700 to 800 words. Both can be used to help market your value as you
navigate your career.

- **Short story** – Write a 200- to 300-word story about a specific
  event in your life related to work. Pick any topic related to a
  job, project, or experience in your life and make sure you have
  a point to the story.
- **Long story** – Write a 700- to 800-word story about
  something you learned reflecting back upon an experience.
  Relate that lesson to work or your value. Employers often
  want to gauge your ability to learn from your experiences, so
  if you have a detailed story in your back pocket you can easily
  tell it anytime.

A few things to keep in mind as you develop your stories:

- Use the first person at a minimum. Too many "I" appearances
  make it a bit tedious for the reader.
- Do not discuss or publish any confidential information.
  When in doubt, leave it out. If you are unsure about

something then figure out another way to tell the story without revealing it.

- Consider publishing both stories on your website.
- Make sure each story has one main point that illustrates why someone would want to hire you.
- Add humor into each story when and where applicable. Being too serious all the time can be a bit draining on people.
- Do not include any client information from work, last names of people, addresses, or anything that would allow a reader to identify someone in your story.
- Do not include any personal, private, or confidential information such as, but not limited to, a mailing address, email address, phone number, client information, financial worksheets, and anything else that should not be disclosed publicly.
- Follow the "when in doubt leave it out" rule
- Make sure everything is spelled correctly
- Have people proofread each story so that they both make sense to an outside reader.

Launch Your Own Web Page

In addition to a detailed LinkedIn profile, a polished résumé, and customized business card, you should also consider creating a personal website to your professional portfolio. A compelling personal website just might give you the edge you need in today's hypercompetitive and challenging job market. As you navigate your career, understand that "56 percent of all hiring managers are more impressed by a candidate's personal website than any other personal branding tool—however, only 7 percent of job seekers actually have a personal website."[5] Think about that for a moment. Less than 10 percent of job seekers are using one of the more effective means of communicating their value. What are you waiting for? Here are some other benefits to creating your personal website:

- You will have greater control over what people will find when they conduct an online search for you. Rest assured that people will search for you. You need to do everything you can in order for people to find the results you want them to read.

- A website allows you to articulate your capabilities much more than a one- or two-page résumé. The more experience you have the more you will have to showcase.
- A personal website is dynamic and interactive and allows you to include photos, videos, blog posts, PDFs, and other files that help you market your value.
- Launching your own web page is a great way to demonstrate how comfortable you are with technology. It also shows potential employers your personality, creativity, and work ethic.

"Thanks to the proliferation of easy-to-use web-based tools and publishing platforms, many of which are free, there's never been a better time to build your own site."[6] Building your website will indeed take time. But the more time you invest in marketing your value the easier it will be to explain it to others when you are navigating your career. Remember, you alone are responsible for helping others understand why they should hire you. When they conduct an online search for you and your personal website appears among the top results, you are positioning your value in a far more compelling fashion than others who lack a site. "Having an informative, well-designed website also sends a message that you take your career seriously—and employers will take note."[7] Take the time to create your website. Moving forward, all you will have to do is edit it as you navigate your career. Remember, marketing your value means explaining what your purpose is to others. A personal website helps tremendously.

Step One: Determine your platform—you have a variety of pay and free options to create your personal website.

- Pay sites: For as little as $10 or less a year, you can purchase your own URL and then a basic website with a limited number of pages. For more information, conduct an online search or use 1and1.com or Godaddy.com. For an example of this type of site, please visit my personal website at www.

michaeledmondsonphd.com. For examples of sites where people merge their personal and business interests together, thus launching their own small business to create multiple revenue streams, please visit http://kathrynbudig.com/ or http://www.danpink.com/

- Free sites: Some companies allow you to set up a website for free. Capabilities vary among the free services, so be sure to check them out and determine which is best for you. For more information, conduct an online search or visit Google Sites, WordPress, or Wix. Examples of free personal brand websites include: http://www.wix.com/clark8310/reliable or http://pascucns.wix.com/ninapascucci

Step Two: Create Your Content—Refer to the exercises you completed in this publication when creating the content for your personal website. Think about what tabs or sections you want on your web page. Sample tabs include but are not limited to:

1. **Résumé**
    a. Include it on your web page and/or as a PDF link.
    b. Be sure to use the résumé format included in this publication as it will highlight your success factors at the top.
    c. DO NOT INCLUDE your phone number or any other contact information on your résumé that you post online.
2. **Personal Statement**
    a. Use the personal statement you created using the exercise in this workbook. This will be important for people to read as they get to know you.
3. **Success Factors**
    a. List the success factors you identified in this publication. This can be done on a separate tab on your website, embedded into your résumé or as part of a portfolio of work you want to display.
4. **Recommendations**
    a. Ask several people to write brief recommendations on your behalf and post online. You should also have these recommendations on your LinkedIn profile if possible.

5. **Pictures**
   a. Take professional headshots so you are represented well. If you have pictures of others on your website, please ask their permission. Be careful of any images or information in the background of a picture as you never want to disclose private or confidential information.

6. **Stories**
   a. Post the short and long stories you created in this workbook. Having those readily available will help others better understand your value. Remember to not disclose any personal, private, or confidential information in your stories. Follow the "when in doubt leave it out" rule.

7. **Work Samples**
   a. Particularly good term papers or assignments that your professors really liked.
   b. Links to places where you interned or volunteered.
   c. Samples of posters presented or articles published.
   d. NOTE: All work samples need to be free of confidential information, so please review and get permission when and where necessary.

8. **Social Network Links**
   a. Be sure profiles on Facebook, LinkedIn, and other social network sites are cleaned up and polished as much as possible prior to launching your web page with links to them. Applications like Social Sweepster can help you clean up your social media accounts.

9. **Other Links**
   a. Think about what else you might want to include when showcasing yourself to other professionals.
   b. Do not disclose any proprietary information from jobs, internships, or other types of work or volunteer experiences.

Considerations when building your website:
   o Keep all language and pictures to a PG rating.
   o Program all links correctly—then double check.
   o Make sure you spell everything correctly.
   o Make sure you use a contact form that is emailed to you.

o Do not post your mailing address, email address, phone number, or any other private contact information on your website.

o Ask people for feedback to make sure site is clear and compelling.

o Triple check your spelling.

o Update your website weekly or monthly.

o Choose colors that are appealing.

o Make sure the font you select is easy to read.

o Have others read it before you publish the site.

o *Do not put your phone number on your website—make sure you remove it from your résumé if you just copy/paste it onto your site.*

CHAPTER 8

Leverage Your Network

Networking is a priority for all professionals regardless of age, location, industry, position, or educational background. Through serendipity and design, networking should be done on a regular basis to extend our web of contacts across geographies, industries, and positions. Networking can help you land a job, earn a promotion, have the lead for an important project, and maintain the position of a valuable asset to your organization and perhaps even industry. To stress the critical importance of networking so as to navigate your career, consider the following three statistics:

- Eighty percent of available jobs are never advertised; so it is important to view networking as a routine function so that you can identify those unadvertised opportunities that could be just what you were looking for.[1]
- The average number of people who apply for any given job is approximately 120. Twenty percent of those applicants get an interview.[2] To get yourself in the mix, complete the other steps in this guide so that you can assess your skills and create a compelling personal brand that you can communicate to others.
- To cut through the clutter of hundreds or even thousands of submissions, "many large and midsize companies have turned to applicant-tracking systems to search résumés for the right skills and experience."[3] Working your network can help get your résumé to a person instead of going through the software where there is a nominal chance of being found.

To better understand your networking capabilities, this chapter contains the following exercises:

- Network audit
- LinkedIn audit
- LinkedIn profile checklist
- Social media audit

Network Audit

1. How many people are you connected to on LinkedIn?
2. How many people are you connected with on Facebook?
3. How many people are you connected with on Twitter?
4. How many people are you connected with on all other social media platforms?
5. How many people are in your professional contact list?
6. How many people are in your personal contact list?
7. How many people do you encounter on a given business day?
8. What is the total number of people in your current network?
9. How many of those are counted more than once? (e.g., the same person who is connected with you LinkedIn is following you on Twitter and is also in your personal contact list)
10. What is the net total number of people in your current network?

Network Audit Example:

1. How many people are you connected to on LinkedIn?   782
2. How many people are you connected with on Facebook?   531
3. How many people are you connected with on Twitter?   0
4. How many people are you connected with on all other social media platforms?   0
5. How many people are in your professional contact list?   348
6. How many people are in your personal contact list?   190
7. How many people do you encounter on a given business day?   75
8. What is the total number of people in your current network?
   1,926

9. How many of those are counted more than once? (e.g., the same person who is connected with you LinkedIn is following you on Twitter and is also in your personal contact list) estimated at 200

10. What is the net total number of people in your current network? 1,726 (1,926–200=1,726)

LinkedIn Audit

LinkedIn is one of the many social networking services offered today. Focused on professional networking, LinkedIn reports over 259 million users in more than 200 countries. "An astounding 94 percent of recruiters used or planned to use social media in their recruitment efforts last year. That's an increase of 16 percent since 2008. And 78 percent of recruiters made a hire through social media in 2013."[4] If you are not on LinkedIn or other critical social media platforms, recruiters will be unable to find you. If they are unable to find you then they cannot contact you for a position. Do you want to take that chance?

1. How often do you check your LinkedIn account?
2. When is the last time you updated your profile?
3. How much time in the last week did you spend networking on LinkedIn? This includes writing recommendations for someone, endorsing them for a professional skill, or asking to be connected for a specific reason?
4. When did you last have someone proof read your profile? You need to make sure you profile is free of typos and grammar mistakes.
5. How many groups have you joined on LinkedIn?
6. When is the last time you participated in a group discussion?
7. Have you tried starting a new group and inviting people into your discussion?
8. When you send a connection request do you personalize the message or just use the default that LinkedIn provides? Consider taking the extra 30 seconds to write a customized message as that is more personable.
9. Have you customized your LinkedIn URL? My address is www. linkedin.com/in/edmondsonphd/. This is far more attractive than

a URL that has numbers and random letters. Remember, you are always presenting your personal brand to strangers, so every little element matters as they search for you, network with you, and establish a professional relationship with you.

10. Professional etiquette suggests that you do not make yourself anonymous while reading other profiles. Making yourself anonymous means that you will be unable to see who visits your profile but consider being as transparent as possible. If you visit someone's profile once or twice that's fine. But exactly why are you hiding your identity when reading profiles? That's an important question to ask and answer as you go about navigating your career.

The 12-Point LinkedIn Profile Checklist

1. Photo: Keep it clean and remember to smile. You can use a good cell phone with a camera since the resolution on most phones these days is rather good. Remember that this is a headshot, so make sure there are no distractions in the background. Professional attire is strongly recommended. Position yourself as someone that looks like others want to work with. Your picture should be of you by yourself. Make sure your picture is free of alcohol or any other questionable substance. Unlike Facebook, your profile picture should not have your pet, family members, or significant others. Remember, recruiters will be studying your picture so please present the most professional image possible.

2. Headline: Help people understand what it is you are looking for. People are busy and if you make them work hard at what it is you do, or what type of position you are looking for, they are more likely to simply move on to the next profile. If you choose your job title, please make sure you are accurate. If your headline reads "Vice President of Product Development," but in reality you are a Director, that is going to be a problem. Only write a headline that is true based on your current situation.

3. Summary: Use the personal statement that you created earlier. Since your statement has 75 words or less, it should all fit into the summary text box on your profile. When you have the same personal statement on your LinkedIn profile, your personal brand website

and your cover letter, you are ensuring that people have a clear, compelling, and concise message about your value.

4. Experience: List the jobs that you held, in reverse chronological order, making sure the most current position is listed first. If you have more than 10 positions, consider publishing a profile that contains only a few of your key experiences. You can always build out the experience part of your personal brand website. When possible, include videos or pictures related to your work experiences.

5. Organizations: Be sure to identify those organizations that you currently belong to. If they are national in scope you may also want to highlight organizations you used to belong to but no longer do. Helping people understand what organizations interest you gives you another way to connect with someone on LinkedIn.

6. Education: Starting with your latest degree, or expected degree, list your educational experiences including off-campus programs, summer programs, and other related events. Some people are comfortable stating their grade point average (GPA) although that is seldom necessary. Be sure to include your major/s and minor/s if applicable.

7. Community Service: List your top three volunteer opportunities and explain the professional skills and personal growth you developed during your experience.

8. Skills and Expertise: With LinkedIn's endorsement function, people that view your profile will see what others believe are your skills and expertise. One interesting exercise is to compare your value proposition with these endorsements. How similar are the words you have chosen to communicate your value to the skills and expertise people have endorsed you for?

9. Honors and Awards: List your honors and awards in reverse chronological order making sure the most current item is listed first. Be sure to explain what the award is, how you were selected, and why you were chosen.

10. Courses: If appropriate, list the undergraduate or graduate courses relevant to your profile at the time.

11. Recommendations: This is perhaps the most important part of your profile. Be sure to ask managers, professors, colleagues, clients, and anyone else who can speak on your behalf. People will be very

interested to read what others had to say about you, so stay current with your recommendations with each passing year.

12. Projects: Be sure to list projects that you led, were a part of, and also completed by yourself. Doing so illustrates your ability to finish what you started. Do not disclose confidential information when listing projects.

Social Media Audit

Today's digital revolution has created hundreds of social media sites that "allow anyone to scale networking efforts more successfully at greater speeds than ever before."[5] Here are 15 of the top social networking sites with an estimated number of unique monthly visitors after each name.[6] For example, Facebook has 900 million unique monthly visitors.

1. Facebook: 900,000,000
2. Twitter: 310,000,000
3. LinkedIn: 255,000,000
4. Pinterest: 250,000,000
5. Google Plus+: 120,000,000
6. Tumble: 110,000,000
7. Instagram: 100,000,000
8. VK: 80,000,000
9. Flickr: 65,000,000
10. Vine: 42,000,000
11. Meetup: 40,000,000
12. Tagged: 38,000,000
13. Ask.fm: 37,000,000
14. Meetme: 15,500,000
15. Classmates: 15,000,000

Questions:

- Which of the 15 social media sites do you belong to?
- Out of those you have an account with, how much time do you spend on each one in a given week?

- How much professional networking are you engaging in on each one?
- Identify your top two or three sites and explain how they help you with networking.
- Do you periodically check your posts for images, pictures, or words that might be offensive or unprofessional? Applications like Social Sweepster can help you clean up your social media accounts.
- When you meet with someone offline, do you connect with them on one of these social media sites?
- Do you have a personal business card that has your LinkedIn or some other social media address on it?
- Does your email signature have your LinkedIn profile link, or some other social media link, on it so people can easily connect with you?

CHAPTER 9

Conduct an Effective Interview

The interview is often the most critical step in the hiring process. After you have completed the previous eight steps, you have a good sense of your life purpose and how to market your value. The only thing left to do is now have a conversation about your life with a complete stranger over an interview. If there is one mistake that most candidates make, it is failing to prepare. The previous eight steps will help you better prepare than almost any other candidate. The last step in marketing your value and navigating your career is to conduct an effective interview so the hiring manager can extend a job offer to you. To leverage all of your work and effort with the previous eight steps, understand the three design elements of an effective interview. First, you need to make sure that the interviewer has no reservations about you. Second, you need to determine if the employer is the right fit for you. And third, if the employer is the right fit for you then you need to demonstrate your interest and verbally state that you want the job. To help you prepare for the interview complete the following exercises:

- The interview checklist
- The panel interview checklist
- The potential interview questions
- Questions you need to ask

Interview Checklist

1. Complete the previous eight steps to assess your skills, traits, and experiences and build a compelling personal brand that you can communicate during the interview.

2. Remain professional at all times. Stay away from using language reserved for friends. The person conducting the interview is not your friend. Even if you have a friendly relationship with the person it is recommended that you maintain the highest level of professionalism at all times during the interview.

3. Be polite to everyone you encounter from the time you enter the parking lot until the time you leave. You have no idea who you will encounter along the way so be overly polite and courteous to every single person.

4. Dress professionally regardless of position, industry, or location. It is your responsibility to present yourself in a neat, polished, and clean manner.

5. When appropriate, present yourself with a firm handshake. It is customary to wait for the one conducting the interview to extend their hand first. That gives you the signal that it is okay to shake their hand.

6. When answering questions, be brief and direct. If you are unsure if you answered the question, feel comfortable enough to ask "Did my response answer your question?"

7. The very last thing you discuss is salary and benefits. This is done only, and let me emphasize, only here, when an offer has been proposed. At that point in time it is appropriate to discuss salary and benefits.

8. Have three questions ready to ask the person or committee conducting the interview: 1)What are your needs as an organization and how does this position address those needs? 2) Six months from now what are you hoping the person in this position has accomplished? 3) How does this position fit in with the other functional areas in the department, division, or organization?

9. Maintain direct eye contact with the interviewer. Remain confident throughout the interview and when in doubt, pause for a moment to answer a question. Sit still and relax. The last thing you want to do is distract the interviewer by moving around in your seat.

10. Smile. Don't be so uptight that you forget to smile. Remember, the person or committee conducting the interview is asking themselves "Can I work with this person each day?" If you are so nervous that you forget to smile that could give off a signal that you are unable to

control your nerves. Go on as many mock interviews as you can to prepare for those that count most.

11. Develop questions that demonstrate your interest and knowledge in working with the company. You must refer to the organization's website and mention several key items you learned during your research.

12. Send a thank you email to all individuals with whom you interviewed. Be sure to get as many business cards as you can.

13. Be aware of your language. Avoid vocal fillers such as "like" or "um". When answering questions, smile and be pleasant but maintain professionalism. You are not performing in a stand-up comedy routine.

14. Answer questions promptly but do not rush into an answer. If need be, count to 10 prior to answering. Any longer and you risk losing your listener.

15. Make sure you have a complete job description prior to the interview. If you do not have one, call the organization. You need to have a clear idea of what is expected of someone in this position.

16. Be enthusiastic about the organization, its mission, and most importantly, the position. Include a copy of the mission in your preparation packet of material.

17. Be prepared. As Abraham Lincoln once said: "Give me six hours to chop down a tree and I will spend the first four sharpening the axe." A good rule of thumb is to prepare at least 3 hours for each interview. The higher the position the more time you will need to prepare; so plan accordingly. A lack of planning will become clear just a few minutes into the interview.

18. When asked the question "Tell me about yourself," refer to the work you have completed in the previous chapters. Start with your success factors and mention your value proposition. Then measure the response by the person or committee conducting the interview. If they ask questions answer them. If they remain quiet, they want you to continue; so focus on the first success factor and explain the value of that experience in the development of your professional skills.

19. It's common to ask for 24 hours before you accept or decline a position. Do not negotiate salary or benefits at this time. Wait until you have slept on it. Doing so demonstrates to the organization that you have given their offer some thought.

20. You must ask questions about the position, organization, and culture. Not asking questions often demonstrates a lack of preparation or thought.

21. Have copies of your résumé with you. Make sure you have a heavy folder or binder that can hold the copies without folding them. If possible, have your résumé printed out on card stock or résumé paper. Remember, the résumé is just one of the many items you have at your disposal to communicate your value so make sure you have it well-prepared prior to the interview.

22. Arrive to the area 30 minutes prior to your interview. Go relax at a hotel lobby or at a local coffee shop or fast-food restaurant. Watching people is a good way to take your mind off of the interview. Depending upon the size of the building you need to navigate, arrive at the front door 10 minutes prior to the interview time. Do not arrive late. If there was an accident, however, and the authorities have closed down the road you were traveling, or even if you get lost, call the office and tell them the truth. If you arrive late and then say there was an accident it looks like you are just trying to come up with a reason as to why you are late.

23. Be as honest and transparent as you can without hindering your chances of landing a job offer. If you get asked "why do you want to leave your current job, what's wrong with it?, simply say that the position you are interviewing for is a far greater fit for your skill set and offers a challenging role that you would like to invest your time and energy into so as to help the organization move forward. Be positive at all times.

24. When filling out a job application, make sure you read and follow the instructions carefully. If you have questions, ask the human resources officer or hiring manager.

25. Use as many resources as you can to prepare. These include attending a workshop, reading a book, using an online resource, or talking to others.

26. Listen carefully to the questions that are being asked. If you need clarification, ask. The more you can create a conversation the better off you are in the interview.

27. Ask for the interviewer's business card so that you will have the proper spelling of his or her name as well as job title, address, and phone number.

28. Even if you think you were spectacular during the interview, continue searching until you have accepted a job offer.

29. Be patient during the interview process. You may be asked to attend more than one interview before a job offer is put on the table. Generally speaking, the higher the position the longer the interview process.

30. If you get the impression that the interview is not going as planned, don't show your disappointment; remain calm. Remember, the people who are interviewing you are busy and have personal issues and professional concerns unrelated to your interview. A lot is on their mind so be sure to demonstrate empathy and ask them how they are doing.

31. Understand that the purpose of sending a résumé is to get a first interview. The purpose of the first interview is to get a second interview. The purpose of the second interview (and perhaps others) is to get a job offer. The purpose of the job offer is to negotiate. And the purpose of negotiation is to agree upon the terms of employment. Landing a job is a process. It is a marathon not a sprint.

32. Be your authentic self. If you have completed all of the exercises in this book you will have a good sense of your purpose, your skills, and the value you can bring to the organization. Be yourself and let people get to know you on the professional level. The last thing you want to do is be someone other than yourself during the interview. If you get the job and then show up as someone else, that could cause problems. The easiest thing to do is to be your authentic self.

33. Don't speak negatively about your present or past employer. Any negative talk about others can only hurt you and will come off as very unprofessional. Make sure all of your social media accounts are clean and free of negative talk. As a good rule of thumb, you should never publish anything negative about a colleague, manager, or organization in which you work.

34. Ask if you may write down notes. Therefore, bring paper and two pens. Don't spend the entire time writing. Just jot down those few

items that you absolutely need to do for a follow-up or make a note of moving forward.

35. At the end of the interview, ask the interviewer what the next step will be. If you feel as though it would be a good fit, ask for the job. If not, or if you are unsure, don't say you want the job. Just thank people for their time and tell them it was great to learn about their company and the opportunity.

Panel Interview Checklist

While many interviews are with one or two people, you need to be prepared for the panel interview. With a minimum of three people, the panel interview presents several challenges you need to understand. During one interview panel, I had breakfast with eight members of a president's cabinet. Below are some things I used to prepare for that panel meeting.

- Research the panel members. Hopefully you have been informed of who will be in attendance as that is the proper protocol. If not, then this step is impossible to complete. Let's work off of the assumption that you know the panel members. Spend time researching each panel member and be sure to print out a profile of each. Understand what each member does and how they fit into the position you are interviewing for.
- Create specific questions. You will need to have specific questions prepared for each panelist. If you are running out of time tell the committee that you have questions for each of them and let them decide who you should ask. Asking questions in front of a panel demonstrates your ability to think.
- Connect with each panelist. With multiple people on the panel you will have a variety of personalities to connect with during the interview. The best way to connect with each member is to have a conversation that engages all of the members. You will also have to find a way to engage the quiet panelists. If there is one dominate personality, you will have to

work hard at connecting with each member but it is a critical element of the process to accomplish.

- <u>Bring a preparation portfolio</u>. Print out material from the organization's website and organize it in a binder. Use an index if you have enough material. This will come in handy during your panel interview as you can refer to something. Doing so will demonstrate to the panel that you are well-prepared. Be as specific as possible when referencing the material. It is imperative that you show them your preparation portfolio and refer to it at least once. This can help differentiate you from the other candidates.

Potential Interview Questions

Interviews are won or lost in your preparation. Prepare for each interview like it's the last one you will ever have. Create a binder full of answers to each of these questions as well as other material related to the organization in general and position specifically. Below is a brief list of potential interview questions. Remember three things when answering any question:

- Be concise, clear, and compelling (keep each answer to 2 minutes or less).
- Ask "should I continue" or "does that answer your question?" as a follow up.
- Speak slowly and maintain eye contact.

Basic Interview Questions: If you have completed the exercises in this book you will be ready to answer any of these questions in a concise, clear, and compelling fashion.

- Tell me about yourself.
- What are your top two or three strengths?
- What are your top two or three weaknesses?
- What about this position appeals to you?
- Where would you like to be in 5 years?

- What's your ideal organizational culture?
- What attracted you to this organization?
- Why should we hire you?
- What type of work is least attractive to you?
- What type of work is most attractive to you?
- What were the main responsibilities of your last position?
- Why do you want to leave your present job?
- Are you willing to relocate for this position?
- Do you have any questions for me? (always ask questions – see below for examples)

Behavioral Interview Questions:

- Explain a project that you recently completed.
- When have you gone above and beyond on a project?
- Tell me about a time when you had to give someone difficult feedback. How did you handle it?
- What is your greatest failure, and what did you learn from it?
- What irritates you about other people, and how do you deal with it?
- If I were your supervisor and asked you to do something that you disagreed with, what would you do?
- How do you deal with difficult people?
- How do you deal with difficult situations or issues?
- How do you respond to mistakes you make?
- How do you respond to mistakes others make that you manage?
- What personality traits bother you most about other people?
- Tell me about a time where you had to deal with conflict on the job.
- What's the most difficult decision you've made in the last 2 years and how did you come to that decision?
- Describe how you would handle a situation if you were required to finish multiple tasks by the end of the day, and there was no conceivable way that you could finish them.

Salary Questions:

- What salary are you seeking?
- What's your salary history?
- The salary range for this position is lower than what you are seeking, if offered this position, would you say yes?

Career Development Questions:

- What are you looking for in terms of career development?
- How do you want to improve yourself in the next year?
- What kind of goals would you have in mind if you got this job?

Getting Started Questions:

- When could you start if we were to choose you?
- How would you go about establishing your credibility quickly with the team?
- What do you see yourself doing within the first 30 days of this job?
- If selected for this position, can you describe your strategy for the first 90 days?

General Questions:

- How would you describe your work style?
- What would be your ideal working environment?
- What do you look for in terms of culture—structured or entrepreneurial?
- What techniques and tools do you use to keep yourself organized?
- If you had to choose one, would you consider yourself a big-picture person or a detail-oriented person?
- How do you deal with information overload?
- Who was your favorite manager and why?
- Was there a person in your career who really made a difference?

- What kind of personality do you work best with and why?
- What are you most proud of?
- What do you like to do?
- What is your personal mission statement?
- What are three positive things your last boss would say about you?
- What negative thing would your last boss say about you?
- What three character traits would your friends use to describe you?
- Describe yourself in one word. Why did you choose this word?
- Describe yourself in seven words or less.
- Who has impacted you most in your career and how?
- What is your greatest achievement outside of work?
- What are the qualities of a good leader? A bad leader?
- What's the last book you read?
- What's the best movie you've seen in the last year?
- What do you like to do for fun?

Suggested Questions You Should Ask

To help prospective employers understand your level of interest in the position, ask questions. The more questions you ask the more interest you will showcase. When possible, ask open-ended questions that will give the interviewer time to talk about what is most important to them. It is an absolute necessity to ask at least three questions but no more than five. Here are some suggested questions:

- What professional skills, soft skills, and experiences would make an ideal candidate for this position?
- What keeps you up at night and how would this position help address that issue?
- What do you enjoy most about working here?
- Is this a new position? If so, is there long-term funding in the budget for it?
- Do you have any hesitations about my qualifications?

- Six months from now how will you know if the person you hired has been successful in this position?
- Where do you see this organization 5 years from now?
- What is the next step in this hiring process?

Conclusion

The last few years have witnessed the emergence and growth of social networking sites, 4G, tablets, ubiquitous wireless and web-enabled cell phones, the cloud, and over one million mobile computing applications. Such advancements have created a global network where billions of people do more, communicate more, and connect more. As Thomas Friedman of *The New York Times* noted, "These tools of connectivity and creativity have created a global education, commercial, communication, and innovation platform on which more people can start stuff, collaborate, learn, and make stuff with more people than ever before."[1]

"What's exciting is that this platform empowers individuals to access learning, retrain, engage in commerce, seek or advertise a job, invent, invest, and crowdsource — all online. But this huge expansion in an individual's ability to do all these things comes with one big difference: *more now rests on you*. (emphasis in original)"[2] In his commencement speech to Alfred University, Robert Benmosche, the CEO of AIG, had some tough love for graduates and referred to the "more rests on you" theme when he said: "You have to accept the hand that's been dealt you in life. Don't cry about it. Deal with it."[3] Recognizing the need to be prepared, Benmosche told graduates to "take an opportunity and treat it as if it's the only one that's coming your way, because that actually may be the truth."[4]

Perhaps the best way to "deal with life" and "take whatever opportunity comes your way" is to recognize that you are the entrepreneur of your own life and therefore, everyone, regardless of background, level of education, or employment position, is a work in progress. Great people, like great organizations, are in a state of perpetual growth. But you need to be self-motivated more so than ever. Realize that due to the technology available, the boundaries are all gone. "But if you're not self-motivated, this world will be a challenge because the walls, ceilings, and floors that protected people are also disappearing. Government will do less for you. Companies will do less for you. Unions can do less for you. There will be fewer limits, but also fewer guarantees. Your specific contribution will define your specific benefits much more. Just showing up will not cut it."[5] In the end you need to realize that you are the only one who can make your dreams come true. As Thomas L. Friedman reminded the graduates from Williams College in June 2005:[6]

> *So whatever you plan to do, whether you plan to travel the world next year, go to graduate school, join the workforce, or take some time off to think, don't just listen to your head. Listen to your heart. It's the best career counselor there is. Do what you really love to do and if you don't know quite what that is yet, well, keep searching, because if you find it, you'll bring that something extra to your work that will help ensure you will not be automated or outsourced. It will help make you an untouchable radiologist, an untouchable engineer, or an untouchable teacher.*

During your journey to becoming that untouchable . . . whatever it is you want to do, keep in mind the following 12 traits that disaster survivors have in common as identified by Laurence Gonzales in his book *Deep Survival: Who Lives, Who Dies, and Why.*[7]

1. **Perceive, believe:** If there is any denial, it is counterbalanced by a solid belief in the clear evidence of their senses. In other words, survivors establish a survival mindset immediately. They see opportunity, even the good, in their situation.
2. **Stay calm:** (use humor, use fear to focus) in the initial crisis, survivors use fear, and aren't ruled by it.
3. **Think/analyze/plan:** Survivors quickly organize, set up small manageable tasks. In other words, they're using the STOP (Stop, Think, Observe, Plan) tool.
4. **Take correct decisive action:** Survivors are able to convert thoughts to action. They deal with what they can from moment to moment, hour to hour.

5. **Celebrate successes**: This is important to maintaining motivation and avoiding hopelessness.

6. **Count your blessings**: Be grateful you're alive.

7. **Play**: Sing, play mind games, recite poetry, count things, etc.

8. **See the beauty**: Survivors are attuned to the wonder of the world.

9. **Believe you will succeed**: All the above practices lead to the point where survivors become convinced they will prevail.

10. **Surrender**: Let go of your fear of failing, or in extreme situations, dying. This is the type of thinking John Leach calls: "resignation without giving up. It is survival by surrender."

11. **Do whatever is necessary**: Survivors know their abilities and don't over or under estimate them. They believe anything is possible and act accordingly.

12. **Never give up**: There is always one more thing you can do.

You will find that these traits are very applicable as you market your value and navigate your career to live a life of purpose. I wish you well along your journey.

APPENDIX 1

Reading List – Books

- Arden, Paul. *It's Not How Good You Are, It's How Good You Want to Be* (2003).Arden challenges readers to answer one simple question: how good do you want to be? This publication resembles a pocket "bible" for the talented and timid to make the unthinkable thinkable and the impossible possible.
- Arden, Paul. *Whatever You Think, Think The Opposite* (2006). As a follow-up to the *It's Not How Good You Are* publication, *What You Think* challenges the reader to think differently about a variety of topics. Such a format pushes people to get uncomfortable in their thinking so they can achieve a new level of achievement.
- Cathy, S. Truett. *How Did You Do It, Truett?: A Recipe for Success* (2007).Truett opened his first restaurant, The Dwarf Grill, in 1946. For 20 years he learned how to achieve and sustain the growth of that one restaurant. In 1967 he opened his first Chick-fil-A restaurant and now there are over 1,400 locations around the United States. This 95-page book provides an excellent firsthand account of his recipe for success.
- Christensen, Clayton M. *How Will You Measure Your Life?* (2012) is based on his 2010 speech to the Harvard Business School's graduating students where he offered a series of guidelines for finding meaning and happiness in life. He used examples from his own experiences to explain how high achievers can all too often fall into traps that lead to unhappiness. Christensen challenges the reader to answer questions such as: How do you measure your life, How can I be sure that I'll find satisfaction in my career?, and How can I avoid compromising my integrity—and stay out of jail?
- Coelho, Paulo. *The Alchemist: A Fable About Following Your Dream* (1988). *The Alchemist* is an allegory originally written in Portuguese.

It has sold more than 65 million copies in more than 150 countries, becoming one of the best-selling books in history. This story is about an Andalusian shepherd boy named Santiago who travels from his homeland in Spain to the Egyptian desert in search of a treasure buried in the Pyramids.

- Colvin, Geoff. *Talent Is Overrated: What Really Separates World-Class Performers from Everybody Else* (2008). Colvin provides substantial evidence that proves how top performers in any field—from Tiger Woods and Winston Churchill to Warren Buffett and Jack Welch—are not determined by their inborn talents. Greatness doesn't come from DNA but from practice and perseverance honed over decades. The key is how you practice, how you analyze the results of your progress, and how you learn from your mistakes that enables anyone to achieve greatness.

- Covey, Stephen R. *The 7 Habits of Highly Effective People: Powerful Lessons in Personal Change* (1989). Be Proactive; Begin with the End in Mind; Put First Things First; Think Win/Win; Seek First to Understand, Then to Be Understood; Synergize; and Sharpen the Saw. Covey argues that the seventh habit is one of renewal and continual improvement, i.e., of building one's personal production capability. To be effective, one must find the proper balance between actually producing and improving one's capability to produce.

- Duhigg, Charles. *The Power of Habit: Why We Do What We Do in Life and Business* (2012). Since habits drive approximately 40 percent of our daily decisions, it is important to increase our self-awareness. Doing so allows us to realize that we can indeed change the way we act. At its core, *The Power of Habit* contains an exhilarating argument: The key to exercising regularly, losing weight, raising exceptional children, becoming more productive, building revolutionary companies and social movements, and achieving success is understanding how habits work.

- Dweck, Carol S. *Mindset: The New Psychology of Success*. Examines the two distinct mindsets that drive people to success or failure: fixed and growth. The fixed mindset suggests that people believe they have a limited amount of talent, intelligence, and ability. Success is about proving that they are smart or talented. The growth mindset suggests that people believe they have the ability to continually develop their intelligence, ability, and potential throughout their entire life. Dweck argues that despite what people may think, changing one's mindset is possible.

- Fisher, Ken. *The Ten Roads to Riches: The Ways the Wealthy Got There (And How You Can Too!)* (2009). After spending decades working with wealthy individuals, Fisher compiles a list of the 10 more common roads individuals took to accumulate their riches. Fisher suggests that people can try more than one road once and in fact should expect failures along the way. The key is to try again and differently, fail and then try again. When necessary, one can select another road to travel as well. Either way the book provides an insight and easy-to-read look at richness.

- Fried, Jason and Heinemeier Hansson, David. *Rework* (2010). Challenges the reader to think differently about work in the second decade of the 21st century amidst the ongoing advancements in technology, high-speed Internet connectivity, and mobile communications. A nontraditional and nonacademic guide to creating multiple revenue streams by starting a business while working full time. And no, one does not need to be a workaholic, have lots of money, or rent an office. All one needs to do is stop talking about launching an idea and just start doing it.

- Gardner, Chris. *Start Where You Are: Life Lessons in Getting from Where You Are to Where You Want to Be* (2009). The book is based on Gardner's extraordinary life story from being poor and homeless to becoming a millionaire through hard work, determination, and perseverance. Includes over 40 lessons including "rise to the call and become your own cavalry" and always remember the basics like showing up on time and being professional in every situation.

- Gardner, Daniel. *The Science of Fear: Why We Fear The Things We Shouldn't and Put Ourselves in Greater Danger* (2008). Gardner eloquently argues that we are the healthiest, wealthiest, and longest lived people in history, yet we are increasingly afraid. This is one of the great paradoxes of our time. Part of the answer rests in the fact that there are few opportunities to make money from convincing people they are, in fact, safer and healthier than ever—but there are huge profits to be made by promoting fear. Gardner argues that to protect ourselves against unreasoning fear we must wake up Head and tell it do its job. We must learn to *think hard.*

- Gergen, Christopher and Vanourek, Gregg. *Life Entrepreneurs: Ordinary People Creating Extraordinary Lives* (2008). The authors interview over 50 entrepreneurs and suggest that the path to a better life for growing numbers of people today is to apply the principles of entrepreneurship (opportunity recognition, innovation, and action) to life itself. Such principles have shifted from the business world to the civic sector and when applied to an individual's life, they can be catalytic and positively transformative.

- Gladwell, Malcolm. *David and Goliath: Underdogs, Misfits, and the Art of Battling Giants* (2013). Challenges the reader to think differently about advantages vs. disadvantages; assumptions vs. reality; the best vs. right decision, and a variety of other key issues related to personal growth. With detailed research he demonstrates how much of what is beautiful and important in the world arises from what looks like suffering and adversity. One learns that effort can trump ability and that conventions are made to be challenged.

- Gladwell, Malcolm. *Outliers: The Story of Success* (2011). Gladwell argues that successful people require 10,000 hours of practice, usually 7 to 10 years, if they wish to master a specific task. The usual suspects of a successful person, intelligence and ambition, actually play a secondary role to the 10,000-hour rule, family, birthplace, and even birth date.

- Gonzales, Laurence. *Deep Survival: Who Lives, Who Dies and Why* (2004). An excellent look into the world of survival. This book is an important read for anyone trying to accomplish anything in life. By reviewing stories that include miraculous endurance and tragic death—how people get into trouble and how they get out again (or not)—*Deep Survival's* examples cover the globe and help us understand the workings of the brain that control our behavior. This is also a great read for those interested in understanding the dynamics of a father–son relationship. Lessons throughout this book can be applied to a variety of individual and organizational situations.

- Harford, Tim. *Adapt: Why Success Always Starts with Failure* (2011). Harford argues that today's challenges simply cannot be tackled with ready-made solutions and expert opinions; the world has become far too unpredictable and profoundly complex. Instead, we must adapt—improvise rather than plan, work from the bottom up rather than the top down, and take baby steps rather than great leaps forward.

- Hoffman, Reid and Ben Casnocha. *The Start-up of You: Adapt to the Future, Invest in Yourself, and Transform Your Career* (2012). In today's challenging and ever changing economy, individuals need to understand that the employer–employee pact is over and traditional job security is a thing of the past. Here, LinkedIn cofounder and chairman Reid Hoffman and author Ben Casnocha show how to accelerate your career in today's competitive world. The key is to manage your career as if it were a start-up business: a living, breathing, growing *start-up of you.*

- Howe, Jeff. *Crowdsourcing: Why The Power of the Crowd is Driving The Future of Business* (2009). This book provides numerous examples on the power of online collaboration never before thought possible. Changing the way people live and work around the world, crowdsourcing describes the process by which the power of the many can be leveraged to accomplish feats that were once the province of the specialized few.

- Kahneman, Daniel. *Thinking, Fast and Slow* (2011). This book describes the two systems that drive the way we think. System 1 is fast, intuitive, and emotional; System 2 is slower, more deliberative, and more logical. Introduces many novel ideas about thinking such as the focusing illusion, which can be summarized as "nothing in life is as important as you think it is when you are thinking about it."

- Kao, John. *Innovation Nation: How America Is Losing Its Innovation Edge, Why It Matters, and What We Can Do To Get It Back* (2007). An interesting and unique view into 21st century innovation that expands its focus to more than just advancements in technology, science, and related fields. Innovation is the ability of individuals, companies, and entire nations to continuously create their desired future and depends on harvesting knowledge from a range of disciplines such as design, social science, and the arts. Additionally, services, experiences, and processes can be just as innovative as products.

- Pink, Daniel. *Drive: The Surprising Truth about What Motivates Us* (2010). Pink argues that high performance and satisfaction—at work, at school, and at home—depends on the deeply human need to direct our own lives, to learn and create new things, and to do better by ourselves and our world. He demonstrates that while carrots and sticks worked successfully in the 20th century, that's precisely the wrong way to motivate people for today's challenges.

- Pryor, Robert and Jim Bright. *The Chaos Theory of Careers: A New Perspective on Working in the Twenty-First Century* (2011). Career development requires that one recognize the instability, disorder, and disequilibrium of today's global marketplace. The complexity of today's global marketplace suggests that life is even more uncertain than we want to admit. Current career development theories lack the sophistication required to help individuals navigate their career. The chaos theory of career development allows people to go transcend what is probable, to understand what is possible when it comes to career opportunities.

- Robinson, Ken. *The Element: How Finding Your Passion Changes Everything* (2009). Provides numerous examples of people who, through intention, accident, or serendipity identified the point at which their natural talent intersects with their personal passion. By creating one's element, people feel inspired to develop themselves. They connect with something fundamental to their sense of identity, purpose, and well-being.

- Sandberg, Sheryl. *Lean In: Women, Work and the Will to Lead* (2013). A well-received book, and now a nonprofit organization after the same name, which examines the challenges women face in trying to get ahead. Sandberg details a variety of strategies that women can incorporate into their personal and professional lives to lean in and take charge of their careers. One attractive element of the book is her willingness to admit her own failings and self-doubt.

- Tapscott, Don and Anthony D. Williams. *Macrowikonomics: Rebooting Business and the World* (2010).Examines how the growing accessibility of information technologies puts the tools required to collaborate, create value, and compete at everybody's fingertips. These advancements are disrupting many institutions that are stuck in the past and unable to move forward. And yet, in every corner of the globe, a powerful new model of economic and social innovation is sweeping across all sectors—one where people with drive, passion, and expertise take advantage of new web-based tools to get more involved in making the world more prosperous, just, and sustainable.

- Toffler, Alvin and Toffler, Heidi. *Revolutionary Wealth: How It Will Be Created and How It Will Change Our Lives* (2006). Another excellent publication by the authors of such previous best sellers such as Future Shock and Third Wave. *Revolutionary Wealth* is a stimulating and provocative look at how the world's economy continues to evolve amidst today's explosion of information production and exchange. The Tofflers argue that in the 21st century wealth is not just about money and must include the "third job"—the unnoticed work people do without pay and its subsequent implications on the way people live and work around the world.

- Turner, Ted. *Call Me Ted* (2008). An extraordinary look at one of the 20th century's most influential entrepreneurs, innovators, and philanthropists. This very personal story provides a valuable set of lessons for anyone looking to succeed. Particularly touching are the stories Turner shares about his father who once told him "Son, you be sure to set your goals so high that you can't possibly accomplish them in one lifetime. That way you'll always have something ahead of you. I made the mistake of setting my goals too low and now I'm having a hard time coming up with new ones." Turner recalls that conversation among many and details how the impact of his father's suicide had on him as a young man.

APPENDIX 2

Reading List – Articles

Internships

- Melissa Korn, "Internships are Increasingly the Route to Winning a Job," *Wall Street Journal*, June 5, 2013. http://online.wsj.com/articles/SB10001424127887324423904578525431344927240
- Amy Scott, "Internships Become the New Job Requirement," *Marketplace*, March 4, 2013.http://www.marketplace.org/topics/economy/education/internships-become-new-job-requirement
- Susan Adams, "Odds are Your Internship Will Get You a Job," *Forbes*, July 25, 2012.http://www.forbes.com/sites/susanadams/2012/07/25/odds-are-your-internship-will-get-you-a-job/
- Dan Kadlec, "Global Internships. The New Key to Getting a Job," *Time*, February 4, 2014. http://time.com/4116/global internships-the-new-key-to-getting-a-job/
- Katharine Hansen, "College Students: You Simply Must Do an Internship (Better Yet: Multiple Internships)!" *Quint Careers.* http://www.quintcareers.com/internship_importance.html
- Brian Burnsed, "Degrees are Great, but Internships Make a Difference," *US News*, April 15, 2010. http://www.usnews.com/education/articles/2010/04/15/when-a-degree-isnt-enough
- Jacquelyn Smith, "Internships May be the Easiest Way to a Job in 2013," *Forbes*, December 6, 2012. http://www.forbes.com/sites/jacquelynsmith/2012/12/06/internships-may-be-the-easiest-way-to-a-job-in-2013/
- Penny Loretto, "Is an Internship Really all that Important?" *About Careers.* http://internships.about.com/od/internshiptip1/a/Is-An-Internship-Really-All-That-Important.htm

- Beth Braccio Hering, "Why are Internships so Important?" *CNN*, April 14, 2010. http://www.cnn.com/2010/LIVING/worklife/04/14/cb.why.internships.important/
- Elizabeth Hoyt, "Let's Get Legal: Guidelines for Paid or Unpaid Internships," *Fastweb!*, April 4, 2014. http://www.fastweb.com/career-planning/articles/3764-let-s-get-legal-guidelines-for-paid-or-unpaid-internships
- Jonathan Rodkin, "Skipped Your College Internship? You're Far Less Likely to Get a Job in Business," *Business Week*, August 15, 2014. http://www.businessweek.com/articles/2014-08-15/skipped-your-college-internship-youre-far-less-likely-to-get-a-job-in-business
- Jacquelyn Smith, "Internship Wish List: The 12 Things Students Value Most," *Forbes*, January 18, 2014. http://www.forbes.com/sites/jacquelynsmith/2014/01/08/internship-wish-list-the-12-things-students-value-most/
- Derek Thompson, "The Thing Employers Look for When Hiring Recent Graduates," *The Atlantic*, August 19, 2014. http://www.theatlantic.com/business/archive/2014/08/the-thing-employers-look-for-when-hiring-recent-graduates/378693/
- Caroline Ceniza-Levine, "How to Convert a Summer Internship Into a Full-Time Job," *Time*, July 22, 2014. http://time.com/money/2998853/convert-summer-internship-full-time-job-hired/

Interviews

- Paul Davidson, "Managers to Millennials: Job Interview No Time to Text," *USA Today*, April 29, 2013. http://www.usatoday.com/story/money/business/2013/04/28/college-grads-job-interviews/2113505/
- Miriam Salpeter, "Why Should we Hire you? Responding to the Job-Interview Concern that Underlies all Questions," *Quint Careers*. http://www.quintcareers.com/why_hire_you.html
- Katharine Hansen, "The Unspoken Secrets of Job Interviewing: How Your Nonverbal Presentation and Behaviors Impact the Impression You Make," *Quint Careers*. http://www.quintcareers.com/interviewing_unspoken_secrets.html

- Yatan Ahluwalia, "Tips for the all-Important Business Meet or Job Interview," *Economic Times*, December 8, 2013. http://articles. economictimes.indiatimes.com/2013-12-08/news/44910798_1_file-case-handshake-chair

- Jeff Haden, "The Perfect Job Interview in 8 Simple Steps," *LinkedIn*, November 21, 2012. https://www.linkedin.com/today/post/article/ 20121121171031-20017018-the-perfect-job-interview-in-8-simple-steps

- Bill Cole, "Behavioral Interviewing Techniques: Smart Strategies To Help You Master This Challenging Approach," *Mental Game Coach*, 2014. http://www.mentalgamecoach.com/articles/BehavioralInter-viewingTechniques.html

- Jenny Treanor, "Job Interview Tips: Because a Strong Handshake is Just the Beginning," *Chicago Tribune*, May 14, 2014. http://articles. chicagotribune.com/2014-05-14/business/sns-201405141030--tms--brazenctnbc-b20140514-20140514_1_strong-handshake-millennial-interview

- Lindsey Kesel, "How to Interview: Hawaii's Award-Winning Female Business Owners Share the Inside Scoop," *Huffington Post*, October 13, 2014. http://www.huffingtonpost.com/lindsey-kesel/ how-to-interview-hawaiis-_b_5970188.html

- Sofia Faruqi, "The Art of the Interview," *Huffington Post*, August 8, 2014. http://www.huffingtonpost.com/sofia-faruqi/the-art-of-the-interview_b_5661933.html

- David Jensen, "The Hiring Guru: Follow-up or You've Given Up," *Huffington Post*, August 25, 2014. http://www. huffingtonpost.com/david-jensen/the-hiring-guru-followup-_b_5702995.html

- Eilene Zimmerman, "Before the Job Interview, Do Your Homework," *New York Times*, June 1, 2013. http://www.nytimes. com/2013/06/02/jobs/before-the-job-interview-do-your-home work.html

- Michelle K, "The Importance of Body Language During an Interview," *ResumeEdge*, September 23, 2014. http://www.resumeedge.com/ importance-body-language-interview/

Résumé

- Phyllis Korkki, "Writing a Résumé That Shouts 'Hire Me,'" *New York Times*, February 27, 2010. http://www.nytimes.com/2010/02/28/jobs/28search.html
- Roxanne Hori, "Maximizing Your Résumé's Impact," *Business Week*, October 24, 2012. http://www.businessweek.com/articles/2012-10-24/maximizing-your-r-sum-s-impact
- Liz Wolgemuth, "5 Résumé Mistakes You're Probably Making," *U.S. News*, January 22, 2009. http://money.usnews.com/money/careers/articles/2009/01/22/5-rsum-mistakes-youre-probably-making
- Michelle K, "Secrets to Writing a Great Cover Letter," *ResumeEdge*, October 7, 2014. http://www.resumeedge.com/secrets-writing-great-cover-letter/
- Shawn P, "An Insider Guide to Résumé Writing- 5 Success Secrest," *ResumeEdge*, September 18, 2014. http://www.resumeedge.com/insider-guide-resume-writing-5-success-secrets/
- Jacquelyn Smith, "12 Myths about Writing Your Resume," *Forbes*, April 1, 2013. http://www.forbes.com/sites/jacquelynsmith/2013/04/01/12-myths-about-writing-your-resume/
- Vivian Giang, Melisa Stanger, "How to Write the Perfect Resume," *Business Insider*, November 29, 2012. http://www.businessinsider.in/How-To-Write-The-Perfect-Resume/articleshow/21056267.cms
- Hillary Chura, "How to Write a Résumé: Examples of What Not to Do," *CBS News*, December 21, 2009. http://www.cbsnews.com/news/how-to-write-a-resume-examples-of-what-not-to-do/
- Kerry Hannon, "Want an Unbeatable Résumé? Read These Tips from a Top Recruiter," *Forbes*, August 24, 2011. http://www.forbes.com/sites/kerryhannon/2011/08/24/want-an-unbeatable-resume-read-these-tips-from-a-top-recruiter/
- Vivian Giang, "What Recruiters Look at During the 6 Seconds They Spend on Your Resume," *Business Insider*, April 9, 2012. http://www.businessinsider.in/What-Recruiters-Look-At-During-The-6-Seconds-They-Spend-On-Your-Resume/articleshow/21056137.cms
- Kate Lorenz, "Seven Things to Know Before Writing Your First Resume," *Career Builder*. https://www.experience.com/alumnus/

article?channel_id=Résumés&source_page=home&article_id=article_
1156537802041

Job Searching

- Joshua Waldman, "10 Ways the Job Search has Changed," *Forbes*, July 2, 2013. http://www.forbes.com/sites/nextavenue/2013/07/02/10-ways-the-job-search-has-changed/
- Dawn Rasmussen, "The Secret 'Sauce' to Any Job Search," *CareerRealism*, March 2, 2012. http://www.careerealism.com/job-search-secret-sauce/
- Lou Adler, "The 10 Best Job-hunting Secrets of All Time," *LinkedIn*, September 11, 2013. https://www.linkedin.com/today/post/article/20130911212503-15454-10-things-job-seekers-must-do-to-get-a-better-job
- Kathryn Sollmann, "The 6 Things You are Doing Wrong in Your Job Search," *Huffington Post*, November 6, 2013. http://www.huffington post.com/kathryn-sollmann/the-6-things-you-are-doing-wrong-in-your-job-search_b_4214424.html
- AARP, "Why Tweets, Post and Links Matter to Your Job Search," *AARP*, May 2014. http://www.aarp.org/work/job-hunting/info-2014/job-search-with-social-media.html
- Arnie Fertig, "10 Emerging Job Search Trends, Tips and Tactics," *U.S. News*, March 4, 2014. http://money.usnews.com/money/blogs/out-side-voices-careers/2014/03/04/10-emerging-job-search-trends-tips-and-tactics
- Frank Traditi and C.J. Hayden, "How to Build a Job Search Network from Scratch," *Get Hired Now*, 2005. http://www.gethirednow.com/articles/network_from_scratch.shtml
- Frank Traditi and C.J. Hayden, "Get Your Job Search Organized," *Get Hired Now*, 2005. http://www.gethirednow.com/articles/get_orga-nized.shtml
- Randall S. Hansen, "Job-Hunting Do's and Don'ts," *Quintessential Careers*. http://www.quintcareers.com/dosdonts.html
- Mary Gay Townsend, "7 Tips to Revamp Your Job Search for 2014," *Mashable*, December 22, 2013. http://mashable.com/2013/12/21/job-search-tips-2/

- Andy Kessler, "Job Hunting in the Network Age," *Wall Street Journal*, July 18, 2014. http://online.wsj.com/articles/the-weekend-interview-job-hunting-in-the-network-age-1405724333
- Jack Mollen, "100 Job Search Tips from FORTUNE 500 Recruiters," *EMC²*. http://www.emc.com/collateral/article/100-job-search-tips.pdf

LinkedIn

- William Arruda, "Why LinkedIn Is the Only Personal Branding Resource You Need," *Forbes*, June 10, 2014. http://www.forbes.com/sites/williamarruda/2014/06/10/why-linkedin-is-the-only-personal-branding-resource-you-need/
- Penny Loretto," Why Is LinkedIn Important?" *About Careers*. http://internships.about.com/od/networking/fl/Who-Needs-a-LinkinIn-Profile.htm
- William Arruda, "22 LinkedIn Secrets LinkedIn Won't Tell You," *Forbes*, March 4, 2014. http://www.forbes.com/sites/williamarruda/2014/03/04/22-linkedin-secrets-linkedin-wont-tell-you/
- Stephanie Sammons, "How to Use 'LinkedIn Today' to Build Online Influence," *Wire Advisor*. http://blog.wiredadvisor.com/how-to-use-linkedin-today-to-build-online-influence/
- Richard Feloni, "11 Things You Should Be Doing on LinkedIn but Probably Aren't," *Business Insider*, March 4, 2014. http://www.businessinsider.com/how-to-make-the-most-of-linkedin-2014-2
- Mathew Ingram, "LinkedIn Continues to Evolve as a News Site," *Business Week*, May 9, 2013. http://www.businessweek.com/articles/2013-05-09/linkedin-continues-to-evolve-as-a-news-site
- Sarah Halzack, "LinkedIn has Changed the way Businesses Hunt Talent," *Washington Post*, August 4, 2013. http://www.washingtonpost.com/business/capitalbusiness/linkedin-has-changed-the-way-businesses-hunt-talent/2013/08/04/3470860e-e269-11e2-aef3-339619eab080_story.html
- Charlotte Steentoft, "The CEO's guide to LinkedIn," *Digital Works*, October 23, 2014. http://digitalworks.info/articles/the-ceos-guide-to-linkedin

- Rick Gillis, "LinkedIn is the New Letter of Recommendation," *CIO*, September 16, 2014. http://www.cio.com/article/2607030/job-search/linkedin-is-the-new-letter-of-recommendation.html
- Craig Kanalley, "How to Use LinkedIn Effectively: Josh Turner Shares Tips in Q&A," *Huffington Post*, February 22, 2013. http://www.huffingtonpost.com/craig-kanalley/how-to-use-linkedin-effectively_b_2744857.html
- Joshua Steimle, "Top 3 Tips from a LinkedIn Expert," *Forbes*, August 7, 2013. http://www.forbes.com/sites/joshsteimle/2013/08/07/top-3-tips-from-a-linkedin-expert/
- JD Gershbein, "What the LinkedIn Changes Mean to You," *Success*, August 13, 2013. http://www.success.com/article/what-the-linkedin-changes-mean-to-you

Social Media

- Melanie Trottman, "Watch Those Tweets: The EEOC Looks at Social Media," *Wall Street Journal*, March 18, 2014. http://blogs.wsj.com/atwork/2014/03/18/watch-those-tweets-the-eeoc-looks-at-social-media/
- Kerry Hannon, "Social Media Can Cost You a Job: 6 Solutions," *Forbes*, June 30, 2013. http://www.forbes.com/sites/kerryhannon/2013/06/30/social-media-can-cost-you-a-job-6-solutions/
- Donna Fuscaldo, "Using Social Media for Job Search," *Fox Business*, June 20, 2014. http://www.foxbusiness.com/personal-finance/2014/06/20/using-social-media-for-job-search/
- Melissa Neiman, "Can Ignoring Social Media Kill a Career?" *Bank Rate*. http://www.bankrate.com/finance/personal-finance/can-ignoring-social-media-kill-a-career-1.aspx
- Jay Moye, "How Social Media is Changing the Way People Search for Jobs," *CocaCola Company*, January 3, 2013. http://www.coca-colacompany.com/stories/hire-power-how-social-media-is-changing-the-way-people-search-for-jobs
- Ryan Holmes, "Turning Your Passion Into Your Position: Social Media for the New Job Market," *Huffington Post*, January 27, 2012.

http://www.huffingtonpost.com/ryan-holmes/social-media-jobs_b_1235895.html

- Ryan Holmes, "3 Ways Social Media Can Help You Land a Job (And Keep It)," *Hootsuite*, October 2013. http://blog.hootsuite.com/3-ways-get-a-job/
- Lilach Bullock, "How to Use Social Media to Find a Job," *Social Media Today*, August 9, 2013. http://www.socialmediatoday.com/content/how-use-social-media-find-job
- Alexis Grant, "10 Smart Ways to Use Social Media in Your Job Search," *US News*, December 3, 2010. http://money.usnews.com/money/careers/slideshows/10-smart-ways-to-use-social-media-in-your-job-search
- Miriam Salpeter, "How to Use Social Media to Land a Job," *U.S. News*, April 16, 2014. http://money.usnews.com/money/blogs/outside-voices-careers/2014/04/16/how-to-use-social-media-to-land-a-job
- Susan Adams, "An Expert's Seven Tips for Using Social Media to Get a Job," *Forbes*, August 13, 2013. http://www.forbes.com/sites/susanadams/2013/08/13/an-experts-seven-tips-for-using-social-media-to-get-a-job/
- Andrea Murad, "Tips for Using Social Media to Find Your Next Job," *Fox Business*, September 3, 2014. http://www.foxbusiness.com/personal-finance/2014/09/03/tips-for-using-social-media-to-find-your-next-job/

APPENDIX 3

Online Resources

Resources (videos and publications)

- A Better Interview: http://www.abetterinterview.com/
- Absolutely Abby: http://www.absolutelyabby.com/
- Career Attraction: http://www.careerattraction.com/
- Career Pivot: http://careerpivot.com/
- Career Realism: http://www.careerealism.com/
- Encore: http://www.encore.org/
- Adrants: http://www.adrants.com/
- Coroflot: http://www.coroflot.com/
- Gigaom: https://gigaom.com/
- Levo: http://www.levo.com/
- Mashable: http://mashable.com/
- MediaBistro: http://www.mediabistro.com/
- TweetMyJobs: http://www.tweetmyjobs.com/
- VentureBeat: http://venturebeat.com/

Job Boards (where you can find a job)

- Blogging4Jobs: http://www.blogging4jobs.com/
- Monster: http://www.monster.com
- CareerBliss: http://www.careerbliss.com/
- Career Builder: http://www.careerbuilder.com/
- Experience: http://www.experience.com/entry-level-jobs/
- FirstJob: https://www.firstjob.com/
- Glass Door: http://www.glassdoor.com/index.htm

- Idealist: http://www.glassdoor.com/index.htm
- Internships: http://www.internships.com/student
- Modern Day Nomads: http://www.moderndaynomads.com/
- Salary.com: http://salary.com/
- Simply Hired: http://www.simplyhired.com/
- USA Jobs: https://www.usajobs.gov/
- YouTern: http://www.youtern.com/
- Beyond: http://www.beyond.com/
- Clearance Jobs: https://www.clearancejobs.com/
- Cleared Path: http://www.clearedpath.com/
- College Recruiter: https://www.collegerecruiter.com/
- Culintro: http://culintro.com/
- Dice: http://www.dice.com/
- Diversity Jobs: http://diversityjobs.com/
- Doostang: http://www.doostang.com/
- eFinancialCareers: http://www.efinancialcareers.com/
- Crunch Board: http://www.crunchboard.com/jobs/
- EnergyFolks: https://energyfolks.com/
- Financial Job Bank: http://www.financialjobbank.com/
- Flex Jobs: http://www.flexjobs.com/
- Geebo: http://geebo.com/
- HealthCareJobSite: http://www.healthcarejobsite.com/
- HireFlyer: http://hireflyer.com/
- iCrunchdata: http://www.icrunchdata.com/
- IT Job Pro: http://itjobpro.com/
- JobLux: http://joblux.com/
- Jobs in Logistics: http://www.jobsinlogistics.com/
- Jobs in Manufacturing: http://jobsinmanufacturing.com/
- Jobs in Trucks: http://jobsintrucks.com/
- Stack Overflow Careers: http://careers.stackoverflow.com/
- Taegan Goddard's Political Wire: http://politicalwire.com/
- TalentZoo: http://www.talentzoo.com/
- TechCareers: http://www.techcareers.com/

Government

- Bureau of Labor Statistics: http://www.bls.gov/ooh/
- Occupational Outlook Handbook: http://www.bls.gov/ooh/
- Careers in Government: http://www.careersingovernment.com/

Women

- Career Girl Network: http://careergirlnetwork.com/
- Classy Career Girl: http://www.classycareergirl.com/
- LeanIn: http://leanin.org/
- Levo League: http://www.levo.com/

Social Media

- LinkedIn: https://www.linkedin.com/
- Twitter: https://twitter.com/
- Facebook: http://facebook.com/
- Layoffspace: http://www.layoffspace.com/
- Xing: https://www.xing.com/
- Fast Pitch Networking: http://www.fastpitchnetworking.com/

Services

- Chameleon Résumés: http://chameleonresumes.com/
- Emprove: http://www.cmprovegroup.com/
- Evisors: http://www.evisors.com/
- Inside Jobs: http://www.insidejobs.com/
- Payscale: http://www.payscale.com/mypayscale.aspx
- Professional Direction: http://www.professiondirection.net/
- VetNet: http://www.vetnethq.com/
- GitHub: https://github.com/
- Recruiter Media: http://recruitermedia.com/

It is not the critic who counts; not the man who points out how the strong man stumbles, or where the doer of deeds could have done them better. The credit belongs to the man who is actually in the arena, who strives valiantly; who at the best knows in the end the triumph of high achievement, and who at the worst, if he fails, at least fails while daring greatly, so that his place shall never be with those cold and timid souls who neither know victory nor defeat.

Theodore Roosevelt, Citizenship of a Republic speech[1]

Notes

Introduction

1. International Labour Organization, "Global Employment Trends, 2014," January 21, 2014.

2. Jordan Weissmann, "How Bad Is the Job Market for the College Class of 2014?" *Slate*, May 8, 2014.

3. "Young, gifted and slack," *The Economist,* November 21, 2012.

4. Yukon Huang and Canyon Bosler, "China's Burgeoning Graduates - Too Much of A Good Thing?" *The National Interest,* January 7, 2014.

5. Jason Fried and David Heinemeier Hansson. 2013. *Remote.* New York: Crown Publishing.

6. Alvin and Heidi Toffler. 2006. *Revolutionary Wealth: How it Will be Created and How It Will Change Our Lives.* Borzoi Book.

7. The Life Twist Study: An Independent Report commissioned by American Express, conducted by The Futures Company, 2013.

8. Marianne Williamson. 1992. *A Return to Love: Reflections on the Principles of 'A Course in Miracle.* New York: Harper Collins.

9. ITU Press Release, "2014 ICT Figures," May 5, 2014.

10. Thomas L. Friedman, "A Theory of Everything (Sort Of)," *The New York Times*, August 13, 2011.

11. Agence France Presse, "A 25-Year Timeline of the World Wide Web," *Business Insider*, March 9, 2014.

12. Andy Kessler, "Job Hunting in the Network Age," *The Wall Street Journal,* July 18, 2014.

13. Jeff Selingo. 2013. *College Unbound: The Future of Higher Education and What It Means for Students.* Boston: Houghton Mifflin.

14. Frank Bruni, "Demanding More From College," *The New York Times*, September 6, 2014.

15. Brian Klapper, "Free Yourself from Conventional Thinking." *Harvard Business Review Blog*, May 6, 2013.

16. Wikipedia, s.v. "High Jump," accessed October 19, 2014, http://en.wikipedia.org/wiki/High_jump.

17. Joseph Durso, "Fearless Fosbury Flops to Glory," *The New York Times,* October 20, 1968.

18. Mason Currey. 2013. *Daily Rituals: How Artists Work.* New York:Alfred A. Knopf.

19. John W. Gardner. 2003. *Living, Leading, and the American Dream*. San Francisco: Jossey-Bass.

Chapter 1

1. Frankl, Viktor. 1959. *Man's Search for Meaning*. New York, NY: Buccaneer Books.
2. Sinek, Simon. 2009. *Start with Why: How Great Leaders Inspire Everyone to Take Action*. New York, NY: Penguin Books.
3. "Building Cathedrals and Sending Rockets to the Moon." *What's The Point*, February 13, 2014.
4. Tolle, Eckhart. 1997. *The Power of Now: A Guide to Spiritual Enlightenment*. Vancouver: Namaste Publishing.
5. John Kao. 2007. *Innovation Nation: How America Is Losing Its Innovation Edge, Why It Matters and What We Can Do to GetIt Back*. New York, NY: Free Press.
6. Laurence Gonzales. 2003. *Deep Survival: Who Lives, Who Dies, and Why*. New York, NY: W.W. Norton & Company.
7. "Best Motivational Speech -Secrets to Success, How Bad Do you Want it? {Full Speech}," YouTube video, 14:49. posted by "sheriefh1, May 12, 2012, https://www.youtube.com/watch?v=WTFnmsCnr6g.
8. Paulo Coelho. 2012. *Manuscript Found in Accra*. New York: Knopf.
9. Gaylon Ferguson. 2009. *Natural Wakefulness: Discovering the wisdom We Were Born With*. Boston: Shambhala Publications.
10. "The Newsroom finale 1x10 - The Greater Fool speech," YouTube video, :52, posted by jayzhelle001, November 27, 2012. https://www.youtube.com/watch?v=4KDSyLT9qKc.
11. Chick-fil-A.com, Accessed October 19, 2014, http://www.chick-fil-a.com/Company/Highlights-Sunday.
12. Kim Severson, "S. Truett Cathy, Chick-fil-A Founder, Dies at 93," *The New York Times*, September 8, 2014.
13. Clay Christensen's Milkshake Marketing," *Harvard Business School, Working Knowledge*, February 14, 2011
14. See note 13 above.

Chapter 2

1. The Life Twist Study: An Independent Report commissioned by American Express, conducted by The Futures Company, 2013.

2. David Wallis, "Increasingly, Retirees Dump Their Possessions and Hit the Road," *The New York Times*, August 29, 2014 and Svati Kirsten Narula, "You Should Spend Money on Experiences, Not Things," *CityLab*, August 28, 2014

3. Art Carey. 2013. "Taking the Measure of Happiness." *Philadelphia Inquirer*.

4. See note 1 above.

5. Seth Godin. 2012. *The Icarus Deception: How High Will You Fly?*. Portfolio Penguin.

6. Betty Kelly Sargent, "Surprising Self-Publishing Statistics," *Publishers Weekly*, July 28, 2014.

7. Carol S. Dweck. 2006. *Mindset, The New Psychology of Success: How We Can Learn to Fulfill Our Potential*. New York: Ballantine Books.

Chapter 3

1. Thomas Friedman. 2013. "Need a Job? Invent It." *The New York Times*, March 30.

2. Jason Fried and David Heinemeier Hansson. 2010. *Rework*. New York: Random House.

3. A'Lelia Bundles. 2002. *On Her Own Ground: The Life and Times of Madam C.J. Walker*. New York: Lisa Drew Books.

4. "The Innovator: Jack Dorsey,", YouTube video 13:29 posted by CBS News, March 17, 2013 http://www.youtube.com/watch?v=eKHoTOYTFH8

5. Douglas Martin. 2003. "Kemmons Wilson, 90, Dies; Was Holiday Inn Founder," *The New York Times*.

6. Gary Vaynerchuk. 2009. Crush it! *Why Now is the Time to Cash in on your Passion.* New York: Harper Collins.

7. Chris Gardner. 2006. *The Pursuit of Happyness*. New York: Harper Collins.

8. Feifei Sun, "Coco Chanel," *Time Magazine*, April 2, 2012.

9. Eric Thomas. 2014. "Success: You Have to Want It As Bad As You Want To Breathe." New York: Spirit Reign Publications.

10. "*Flying Machines Which Do Not Fly*" *The New York Times*, October 9, 1903.

11. Nicholas D. Kristof, "His Gift Changes Lives," *The New York Times*, December 16, 2009.

12. Wikipedia, s.v. "High Jump," accessed October 19, 2014, http://en.wikipedia.org/wiki/High_jump.

13. Tim Harford, *Adapt: Why Success Starts with Failure,* (Farrar, Straus and Giroux 2012), pp. 97-101.

14. "About Jimmy," Jimmywales.*com*, http://jimmywales.com/about-jimmy/.

15. "Online Extra: Fred Smith on the Birth of FedEx," *Businessweek*, September 19, 2004.

16. "Why Paul Orfalea Didn't Franchise Kinko's," *Businessweek*, September 23, 1998.

17. Chick-fil-A.com, Accessed October 19, 2014, http://www.chick-fil-a.com/Company/Highlights-Sunday.

18. Sheryl Sandberg, "Why I Want Women To Lean In," *Time Magazine*, March 7, 2013.

19. Wikipedia, s.v. "Dale Chihuly," accessed October 19, 2014, http://en.wikipedia.org/wiki/Dale_Chihuly

20. John Kay. 2010. *Obliquity: Why Our Goals Are Best Achieved Indirectly*. New York: Penguin Books.

21. Wikipedia, s.v. "Michael Wesch," accessed October 19, 2014, http://en.wikipedia.org/wiki/Michael_Wesch

22. Wikipedia, s.v. "Man on Wire," accessed October 23, 2014, http://en.wikipedia.org/wiki/Man_on_Wire.

23. Douglas Martin, "Randy Pausch, 47, Dies; His 'Last Lecture' Inspired Many to Live with Wonder," *The New York Times*, July 26, 2008.

24. Reid Hoffman and Ben Casnocha. 2012. *The Start-up of You: Adapt to the Future, Invest in Yourself, and Transform Your Career*. New York: Crown Publishing.

25. Bernard Marr, "Careful! These 25 Quotes Might Inspire You," *LinkedIn*, May 23, 2013.

26. Maureen O'Connor, "Final Tally: Americans Were 12 Times More Interested in Miley Cyrus Than Syria," *New York Magazine*, September 9, 2013.

27. Mark Wenberger, "On Youth Unemployment, It's Time For Business to Lead," *Forbes*, July 17, 2014.

28. Sarah E. Needleman, "Skills Shortage Means Many Jobs Go Unfilled," *The Wall Street Journal*, July 9, 2014.

29. Melissa Korn, "Bosses Seek Critical Thinking, but What Is That?" *The Wall Street Journal*, October 21, 2014.

30. Tyler Cowen, 2013, *Average is Over: Powering America Beyond the Age of the Great* Stagnation (New York: Plume Books)

31. David Brooks, "The Life Report," *The New York Times*, October 27, 2011.

32. Wikipedia, s.v. "Williams Jennings Bryan," accessed October 25, 2014, http://en.wikiquote.org/wiki/William_Jennings_Bryan

33. Marian Wright Edelman, *The Measure of Our Success: A Letter to My Children and Yours* (Harper Perennial 1992), p.38.

34. Chance Barnett, "Crowdfunding Sites in 2014," *Forbes*, August 29, 2014.

35. Jim Bright and Robert Pryor. 2011. *The Chaos Theory of Careers*. New York: Routledge.

36. Scott Adams. "You Are what You Learn," The Scott Adams blog, October 19, 2011, http://dilbert.com/blog/entry/who_are_you/

Chapter 4

1. Gail McMeekin. "Don't Start a Job Hunt Until You Read This," *Huffington Post College Blog,* May 15, 2013.

2. "Managers to Millennials: Job interview no time to text," *USA Today*, April 29, 2013.

3. See note 2 above.

4. Dorotea Szkolar, "Facebook Hookup Apps: Privacy Disaster Waiting to Happen?" *Information Space*, March 25, 2013.

5. "Hiring Decision in the Age of Social Media," *The Greater Lansing Business Monthly*. n.d.

6. Catherine Skrzypinski. "SHRM Poll: Social Networking Websites Popular as Employer Recruiting Tool," April 18, 2011

7. See note 6 above.

8. "Amazon founder and CEO Jeff Bezos delivers graduation speech at Princeton University," YouTube video, 18:52, posted by Princeton Academics, June 11, 2010. http://www.youtube.com/watch?v=vBmavNoChZc

9. See note 8 above.

10. Ruth Mantell, "Must-have Job Skills in 2013," *Wall Street Journal*, November 18, 2012.

11. Christine Choi, "Top 10 Overused LinkedIn Profile Buzzwords of 2013," LinkedIn article, December 11, 2013.

12. See note 11 above.

13. Susan Adams, "The Best and Worst Words to Use on Your Résumé," *Forbes*, March 17, 2014.

14. Katharine Hansen, "Avoid These 10 Résumé Mistakes," *Quintessential Careers*. n.d.

Chapter 5

1. "Randy Pausch Last Lecture: Achieving Your Childhood Dreams" YouTube video, 76:26, posted by "Carnegie Mellon, December 20, 2007, http://www.youtube.com/watch?v=ji5_MqicxSo

2. Douglas Martin. "Randy Pausch, 47, Dies; His 'Last Lecture' Inspired Many to Live with Wonder," *The New York Times*, July 26, 2008.

3. Wikipedia, s.v. "Jon Hamm," accessed October 19, 2014, http://en.wikipedia.org/wiki/Jon_Hamm.

4. See note 3 above.

5. Zac Bissonnette. "Your College Major May Not be as Important as You Think," *The New York Times*, November 3, 2010. http://thechoice.blogs.nytimes.com/2010/11/03/major/?_r=0

6. See note 1 above.

7. David Brooks. "Tools for Thinking," *The New York Times*, March 28, 2011, http://www.nytimes.com/2011/03/29/opinion/29brooks.html.

8. Debra Humphreys and Patrick Kelly. "Liberal Arts Graduates and Employment: Setting the Record Straight," *Association of American Colleges & Universities*, 2014, http://www.aacu.org/sites/default/files/files/LEAP/nchems.pdf.

9. Amy Scott. "What Do Employers Really Want from College Grads?" *Marketplace Education*, March 4, 2013.

10. Meredith Lepore. "Most Employers Don't Care About What Your College Major Was," *The Grindstone*, June 6, 2011.

11. Jeffrey J. Selingo. "Does the College Major Matter? Not Really," *The New York Times*, April 29, 2013, http://thechoice.blogs.nytimes.com/2013/04/29/does-the-college-major-matter-not-really/?_php=true&_type=blogs&_r=0

12. Council on Competitiveness. "Innovate America: Thriving in a World of Challenge and Change." National Innovation Initiative, Interim Report, July 23, 2004.

13. Dan Schawbel. "Trend: Companies Hire for Cultural Fit Over Qualifications," *The Fast Track*, March 1, 2013.

14. See note 7 above.

15. Mark Salisbury. "We're Muddying the Message on Study Abroad," *The Chronicle of Higher Education*, July 30, 2012.

16. Steve Tomasco. "IBM 2010 Global CEO Study: Creativity Selected as Most Crucial Factor for Future Success," *IBM*, May 18, 2010, https://www-03.ibm.com/press/us/en/pressrelease/31670.wss.

17. Bureau of Labor Statistics. "Number of Jobs, Labor Market Experience, and Earnings Growth: Results from a National Longitudinal Survey News Release," June 27, 2008.

18. See note 12 above.

19. John M. Eger. "It's All About Creativity," *Huffington Post*, March 21, 2012, http://www.huffingtonpost.com/john-m-eger/-its-all-about-creativity_b_1358886.html

20. Jacquelyn Smith. "Internships May be the Easiest Way to a Job in 2013," *Forbes*, December 6, 2012.

21. Meghan Casserly. "Top Five Personality Traits Employers Hire Most," *Forbes Woman*, October 4, 2012.

22. Geoff Colvin. 2008. *Talent Is Overrated: What Really Separates World-Class Performers from Everybody Else*. New York: Penguin Books.

23. Michele Menegay Marion. "Liberal Arts Is Slang for Job Skills," *Ask the Headhunter*, http://www.asktheheadhunter.com/gv980429.htm.

24. Richard Nelson Bolles. "What Color Is Your Parachute," *Ten Speed Press*, August 14, 2012.

25. Nikki Blacksmith and Jim Harter. "Majority of American Workers Not Engaged in Their Jobs," *Gallup Wellbeing*, October 28, 2011. http://www.gallup.com/poll/150383/majority-american-workers-not-engaged-jobs.aspx

26. See note 21 above.

27. Tomas Chamorro-Premuzic. "Does Money Really Affect Motivation? A Review of the Research," *HBR Blog Network*, April 10, 2013, http://blogs.hbr.org/cs/2013/04/does_money_really_affect_motiv.html

28. http://2012books.lardbucket.org/books/exploring-business-v2.0/section_11_03.html

29. Paulo Coelho. 1994. *The Alchemist*. New York: Harper Collins.

30. Lisa Wade. "Two-Thirds of College Students Think They're Going to Change the World," *Sociological Images*, May 20, 2013.

31. Lisa Wade. "Advice for College Grads from Two Sociologists," *Huffington Post*, May 24, 2013.

32. Jeffrey Selingo. "Does the College Major Matter? Not Really?" *The New York Times*, April 29, 2013.

33. Deborah L. Jacobs. "Why A Career Jungle Gym is Better Than A Career Ladder," *Forbes*, March 14, 2013.

34. Jessica Radloff. "Why We Really Obsess Over Celebrities," *Glamour*, August 27, 2013.

Chapter 6

1. Mark Salisbury, "We're Muddying the Message on Study Abroad," *The Chronicle of Higher Education*, July 30, 2012.

2. Mark Gilman, "College Graduates: You're Doing It Wrong, and it's OK." *Huffington Post blog*, July 22, 2013.

3. Erik Brynjolfsson and Andrew McAfee. 2014. *The Second Machine Age: Work, Progress, and Prosperity in a Time of Brilliant Technologies*. New York: W.W. Norton & Co.

4. Bill Taylor, "Are You Learning as Fast as the World is Changing," *Harvard Business Review Blog*, January 26, 2012.

5. Thomas L. Friedman, "The Start-Up of You," *The New York Times*, July 12, 2011.

6. NMC Horizon Report: 2014 Higher Education Edition is a collaboration between the new Media Consortium and the EDUCASUE Learning Initiative, an EDUCASUE Program.

7. MG Siegler, "Eric Schmidt: Every 2 Days We Create as Much Information as We Did Up to 2004," *Tech Crunch,* August 4, 2010.

8. "Global mobile statistics," posted on Mobiforge.com, May 2, 2014.

9. Juliette Garside, "OMG! Number of UK Text Messages Falls for First Time," *The Guardian*, January 12, 2014.

10. Don Tapscott and Anthony D. Williams. 2008. *Wikinomics: How Mass Collaboration Changes Everything*. New York: Penguin Books.

11. See note 10 above.

12. Top 20 Internet Countries as of December 31, 2013, Internet World Stats.

13. Mark Walsh, "Pew: Most Will Access Internet via Mobile by 2020," *Online Media Daily*, December 15, 2008.

14. Andrew C. Revkin, "U.N.: Young and Old Boom on the Road to 9 Billion," *New York Times,* March 11, 2009.

15. Carolyn Duffy Marsan, "10 Fool-Proof Predictions for the Internet in 2020," *PC World*, January 5, 2010.

16. Michael T. Fralix. 2001. "From Mass Production to Mass Customization," *Journal of Textile and Apparel, Technology and Management* 1(2).

17. Thomas L. Friedman. 2005. *The World Is Flat: A Brief History of the Twenty-First Century*. New York: Farrar, Straus and Giroux.

18. "Self-publishing Movement Continues Strong Growth in U.S., says Bowker," Bowker press release, October 9, 2013.

19. David Brooks, "The Triumph of Hope Over Self-Interest," *The New York Times*, January 12, 2003.

20. Laura Tyson, "Why Are U.S. Workers Being Left Behind," *World Economic Forum blog*, September 30, 2014.

21. Robert Gebeloff and Shaila Dewan, "Measuring the Top 1% by Wealth, Not Income," *The New York Times*, January 17, 2012.

22. Jim Clifton. 2011. *The Coming Jobs War.* New York: Gallup Press.

23. See note 22 above.

24. Jacob Goldstein and Lam Thuy Vo, "22 Million Americans Are Unemployed or Underemployed," *NPR blog*, April 4, 2013.

25. Annalyn Censky, "How the middle class became the underclass," *CNN Money,* February 16, 2011.

26. Steven Greenhouse, "Our Economic Pickle," *The New York Times,* January 12, 2013.

27. See note 26 above.

28. Jerry Geisel, "Fewer Employers offering Defined Benefit Pension Plans to New Salaried Employees," *Workforce*, October 3, 2012.

29. See note 28 above.

30. Ed Gandia, *2012 Freeland Industry Report: Data and Analysis of Freelancer Demographics, Earnings, Habit and Attitudes*, August 2012.

31. See note 30 above.

32. Neil Shah, "Nearly One in 10 Employees Works from Home," *The Wall Street Journal*, March 5, 2013.

33. Kenneth Rapoza, "One in Five Americans Work from Home, Numbers Seen Rising Over 60%," *Forbes*, February 18, 2013.

34. See note 33 above.

35. Danielle Kurtzleben, "Nearly 2 million Americans work multiple part-time jobs to make ends meet," *Vox*, October 3, 2014.

36. Susan Adams, "Most Americans Are Unhappy at Work," *Forbes*, June 20, 2014.

37. David Leonhardt and Kevin Quealy, "The American Middle Class Is No Longer the World's Richest," *The New York Times*, April 22, 2014.

38. Ben Casselman, "The American Middle Class Hasn't Gotten A Raise in 15 years," FiveThirtyEight, September 22, 2014

39. Accenture 2013 College Graduate Employment Survey released April 29, 2013.

40. Kimberly Gedeon, "New Report Says 62% of America's jobs Pay Less than $20 Per Hour," *Madame Noire*, April 7, 2014.

41. Wikipedia, s.v. "Personal Household Income," accessed October 19, 2014, http://en.wikipedia.org/wiki/File:Personal_Household_Income_U.png

42. See note 41 above.

43. See note 41 above.

44. See note 41 above.

45. How 401(k)s are failing millions of Americans," *The Week*, April 20, 2012.

46. See note 45 above.

47. Melanie Hicken, "31% of Americans have no retirement savings at all," *CNN Money*, August 8, 2014.

48. Brian Fippinger, "The Job of a Lifetime, No Longer Lasts a Lifetime," *Social Hire*, May 24, 2013.

49. Emily Jane Fox, "260,000 Graduates in Minimum Wage Jobs," *Money*, March 31, 2014.

50. Stacey Patton, "The PhD. Now Comes with Food Stamps," *The Chronicle of Higher Education*, May 6, 2012.

51. "Positive Uncertainty: A New Decision Making Framework for Counseling," *Journal of Counseling Psychology*, 1989.

52. Carl Benedikt Frey and Michael A. Osborne, "The Future of Employment: How Susceptible Are Jobs to Computerization?" September 17, 2013.

53. H.B. Gelatt, "Positive Uncertainty: A Paradoxical Philosophy of Counseling Whose Time Has Come," ERIC Clearinghous eon Counseling and Personnel Services, December 1992.

54. The Life Twist Study: An Independent Report commissioned by American Express, conducted by The Futures Company, 2013.

55. Mihaly Csikszentmihalyi. 1990. *Flow: The Psychology of Optimal Experience.* New York: Harper Collins.

56. Ralph Ellison. 1947. *Invisible Man.* New York: Signet Books.

Chapter 7

1. John Michael Morgan. 2011. *Brand Against the Machine: How to Build Your Brand, Cut Through the Marketing Noise, and Stand Out from the Competition.* Hoboken, NJ: John Wiley.

2. Gary Vaynerchuk. 2009. *Why Now Is The Time To Crush It! Cash In On Your Passion.* New York: Harper Studio.

3. Jim Loehr. 2007. *The Power of Story: Change Your Story, Change your Destiny in Business and in Life.* New York, NY: Free Press.

4. Christopher Bowe, "Reinvent Your Career by Writing Your Own Narrative," *Harvard Business Review* blog, May 4, 2012.

5. Jacquelyn Smith, "Why Every Job Seeker Should Have a Personal Website, And What It Should Include," *Forbes*, April 26, 2013.

6. Nancy Collamer, "Beyond LinkedIn - Why You Need Your Own Website For A Job Search," *Forbes*, September 30, 2013.

7. See note 5 above.

Chapter 8

1. Jen Hubley Luckwaldt, "80 Percent of Job Openings Aren't Advertised," *PayScale*, March 25, 2013.

2. Jacquelyn Smith, "7 Things You Probably Didn't Know About Your Job Search," *Forbes*, April 17, 2013.

3. Lauren Weber, "Your Résumé vs. Oblivion," *The Wall Street Journal,* January 24, 2012.

4. Mindy Thomas, "If You Want a New Job, Cover All Your Bases," LinkedIn, August 5, 2014.

5. Brian Honigman, "5 Strategies for Effective Networking in the Digital Age," Adknowledge blog, January 16, 2014.

6. "Top 15 Most Popular Social Networking Sites," ebizmba.com, October 2014.

Chapter 9

1. Thomas L. Friedman, "It's a 401(k) World," *The New York Times*, April 30, 2013.

2. See note 1 above.

3. Zachary Tracer and Noah Buhayar, "AIG CEO Tells Grads Don't Cry About Economy, Deal With It," *Bloomberg*, May 14, 2013.

4. See note 3 above.

5. See note 1 above.

6. Thomas L. Friedman, "Listen to Your Heart," Humanity.org, June 5, 2005.

7. Laurence Gonzales. 2003. *Deep Survival: Who Lives, Who Dies, and Why.* New York: W.W. Norton & Company.

Appendix

1. Wikipedia, s.v. "Citizenship in a Republic," accessed October 25, 2014, http://en.wikipedia.org/wiki/Citizenship_in_a_Republic

Index

OTHER TITLES IN THE HUMAN RESOURCE MANAGEMENT AND ORGANIZATIONAL BEHAVIOR COLLECTION

- *Manage Your Career: 10 Keys to Survival and Success When Interviewing and on the Job* by Vijay Sathe
- *Developing Employee Talent to Perform: People Power* by Kim Warren
- *Culturally Intelligent Leadership: Leading Through Intercultural Interactions* by Mai Moua
- *Letting People Go: The People-Centered Approach to Firing and Laying Off Employees* by Matt Shlosberg
- *The Five Golden Rules of Negotiation:* by Philippe Korda
- *Cross-Cultural Management* by Veronica Velo
- *Conversations About Job Performance: A Communication Perspective on the Appraisal Process* by Michael E. Gordon and Vernon Miller
- *How to Coach Individuals, Teams, and Organizations to Master Transformational Change Surfing Tsunamis* by Stephen K. Hacker
- *Managing Employee Turnover: Dispelling Myths and Fostering Evidence-Based Retention Strategies* by David Allen and Phil Bryant
- *Mastering Self-Motivation: Bringing Together the Academic and Popular Literature* by Michael Provitera
- *Effective Interviewing and Information Gathering: Proven Tactics to Improve Your Questioning Skills* by Tom Diamante
- *Managing Expatriates: Return on Investment Approach* by Yvonne McNulty and Kerr Inkson
- *Fostering Creativity in Self and the Organization: Your Professional Edge* by Eric W. Stein
- *Designing Creative High Power Teams and Organization: Beyond Leadership* by Eric W. Stein
- *Creating a Pathway to Your Dream Career: Designing and Controlling a Career Around Your Life Goals* by Tom Kucharvy
- *Leader Evolution: From Technical Expertise to Strategic Leadership* by Alan Patterson
- *Followership: What It Takes to Lead* by James H. Schindler
- *The Search For Best Practices: Doing the Right Thing the Right Way* by Rob Reider

Announcing the Business Expert Press Digital Library

Concise e-books business students need for classroom and research

This book can also be purchased in an e-book collection by your library as

- a one-time purchase,
- that is owned forever,
- allows for simultaneous readers,
- has no restrictions on printing, and
- can be downloaded as PDFs from within the library community.

Our digital library collections are a great solution to beat the rising cost of textbooks. E-books can be loaded into their course management systems or onto student's e-book readers. The **Business Expert Press** digital libraries are very affordable, with no obligation to buy in future years. For more information, please visit **www.businessexpertpress.com/librarians**. To set up a trial in the United States, please contact **sales@businessexpertpress.com**.

CPSIA information can be obtained
at www.ICGtesting.com
Printed in the USA
FFOW04n0318150415
12593FF

9 781631 572180